INVENTIONS AND OFFICIAL SECRECY

INVENTIONS AND OFFICIAL SECRECY

*A History of Secret Patents
in the United Kingdom*

T. H. O'DELL

CLARENDON PRESS · OXFORD
1994

Oxford University Press, Walton Street, Oxford OX2 6DP
Oxford New York
Athens Auckland Bangkok Bombay
Calcutta Cape Town Dar es Salaam Delhi
Florence Hong Kong Istanbul Karachi
Kuala Lumpur Madras Madrid Melbourne
Mexico City Nairobi Paris Singapore
Taipei Tokyo Toronto
and associated companies in
Berlin Ibadan

Oxford is a trade mark of Oxford University Press

Published in the United States
by Oxford University Press Inc., New York

British Library Cataloguing in Publication Data
Data available

Library of Congress Cataloging in Publication Data
Data available

ISBN 0-19-825942-5

1 3 5 7 9 10 8 6 4 2

Typeset by Graphicraft Typesetters Ltd., Hong Kong
Printed in Great Britain
on acid-free paper by
Bookcraft Ltd., Midsomer Norton, Avon

Contents

List of Figures   viii

List of Abbreviations   ix

Acknowledgements   x

1   Introduction   1

2   The First Secret Patent   4

2.1	John Macintosh	4
2.2	Patent No. 1774 of 1855	5
2.3	The Old Law	9
2.4	The 1829 Select Committee	11
2.5	The Great Exhibition	13
2.6	The 1851 Select Committee	15
2.7	A Change of Government	16
2.8	The Act of 1852	17

3   The Secret Patents Act of 1859   19

3.1	Munitions of War	19
3.2	William Armstrong	20
3.3	The Commissioner's Report of 1864	22
3.4	The Abolitionists	25
3.5	The Copyright Analogy	30
3.6	The Abolitionists Defeated	32

4   Towards an Official Secrets Act   35

4.1	Public Records	35
4.2	C. M. Clode Draws up a Paper	36
4.3	Real Estate	37
4.4	Secrecy	38
4.5	The Act of 1883	40
4.6	Secrecy in the Act of 1883	43
4.7	The Official Secrets Act of 1889	44
4.8	Conclusions	48

5   The Secrets of Two Technical Revolutions   49

    5.1   The Beginnings of Wireless Telegraphy   49
    5.2   Marconi's Letter to the War Office   50
    5.3   Marconi's Patent No. 12039 of 1896   53
    5.4   Examination by Men of Scientific Eminence   57
    5.5   A Technical Revolution in the Air   58
    5.6   Fathering the Unthinkable   60

6   Introducing the Examiners   62

    6.1   A Question in the House   62
    6.2   The Committee of the Board of Trade   63
    6.3   The Act of 1902   66
    6.4   The Acts Conflict   67
    6.5   The Patent Act of 1907   69
    6.6   The Great War   70
    6.7   Peace   74

7   Between the Wars   79

    7.1   A Committee of the Privy Council   79
    7.2   Rewards for Inventors   80
    7.3   The Disclosure of Colonel Clark   81
    7.4   The Case of the Autopilot   84
    7.5   The Boulton Paul Case   86
    7.6   The Case of Leo Szilard   88
    7.7   Time for a Change   90

8   The Second World War   95

    8.1   The Health of the State   95
    8.2   DORA   96
    8.3   The Scientific Advisory Committee   97
    8.4   Radar   99
    8.5   The Cavity Magnetron   100
    8.6   E. C. S. Megaw   102
    8.7   The Magnetron Secret Patents   104
    8.8   Problems with the Magnetron Patents   105
    8.9   Awards to Inventors   106
    8.10 The Dambusters   108
    8.11 Conclusions   111

9 Making Wartime Procedure Permanent   113

  9.1 The Atomic Bomb   113
  9.2 The McMahon Act of 1946   114
  9.3 The Atomic Energy Act of 1946   115
  9.4 An Unusual Debate   116
  9.5 Preparing for a Change   119
  9.6 The Patents and Designs Bill of 1949   121
  9.7 The Case of the Hovercraft   123
  9.8 The Early Hovercraft Patents   124
  9.9 The National Research and Development
       Corporation   126

10 The Last Secret Patent   129

  10.1 Closed until 2007   129
  10.2 The Patents Act of 1977   130
  10.3 The 1977 Bill in Parliament   131
  10.4 A Secret Obsession   134

References   140

Index   145

Figures

1 First two pages of John Macintosh's patent
   specification, BPN 1774 of 1855   6
2 Drawings from William Armstrong's patent
   specification, BPN 779 of 1858   21
3 Last two pages of Robert Feather's amended
   disclaimer   28
4 (*a*) Figure from Marconi's specification, BPN 12039
       of 1896   54
   (*b*) Simplification of Marconi's figure showing the
       feedback path   55
5 Diagram from the specification of BPN 206537   77
6 (*a*) First page of Leo Szilard's secret patent
       specification, BPN 630726   91
   (*b*) First page of Leo Szilard's specification for
       BPN 440023   92
7 Drawings in specification, BPN 588185, published
   May 1947, showing construction of cavity magnetron
   manufactured at GEC Wembley laboratories in 1941   103
8 First page of specification, BPN 937959, Sir Barnes
   Wallis's bouncing bomb   110

Abbreviations

BPN	British Patent Number(s)
BPP	British Parliamentary Papers
CPJ	*Commissioners of Patents' Journal*, 1–3130 (1854–83)
*EB*11	*Encyclopaedia Britannica*, eleventh ed., vols. 1–28
ERO	Essex Record Office, Chelmsford
H2	Hansard, second series, vols. 1–21 (1803–30)
H3	Hansard, third series, vols. 1–356 (1830–91)
H4	Hansard, fourth series, vols. 1–199 (1892–1908)
IOJ(P)	*Illustrated Official Journal (Patents)*, 1–2195 (1889–1931)
HPC	P. A. Hayward (1987–8). *Hayward's Patent Cases*, vols. 1–11. Professional Books, Abingdon.
OJ(P)	*Official Journal (Patents)*, 2196– (1931–)
PDC	*Parliamentary Debates (Commons)*, vol. 1– (1909–)
PDL	*Parliamentary Debates (Lords)*, vol. 1– (1909–)
PRO	Public Record Office, London and Kew

Acknowledgements

I would like to thank the staff at the British Library of Political and Economic Science for allowing me access to their main collection and for the many occasions when they have helped me to find what I was looking for. The same thanks are due to the staff at the Science, Technology and Patents Branch of the British Library at Southampton Buildings, the Science Museum Library at South Kensington, and the Public Record Offices at Chancery Lane and at Kew.

Some points that puzzled me were cleared up by visits to the Greater London Record Office, in Northampton Road, and the Essex Record Office at Chelmsford. In both places the staff were most helpful. Correspondence with the National Museum of Labour History, in Manchester, and with the Library of the Royal Aeronautical Society, produced prompt answers to my queries for which I am most grateful.

The extracts from patent specifications, which have been used as illustrations in this book, have been reproduced by permission of Her Majesty's Stationery Office, Publication Division (Copyright), at Norwich. Where Crown Copyright is still in force the illustration is marked accordingly. Permission to publish the text of Marconi's letter to the War Office was kindly given by GEC-Marconi Ltd., who own the copyright. The original letter itself is the property of Her Majesty's Government and is in the custody of the Public Record Office at Kew. The full PRO reference is given in Chapter 5.

Professor David Vaver, Professor of Law at Osgoode Hall Law School, York University, Ontario, and Editor in Chief of the *Intellectual Property Journal*, where I published the results of my first research on secret patents (*IPJ* 7 at 321–31), was a source of great encouragement to me at the start of this work, and I would also like to thank him for his advice during my search for a publisher, which eventually led me to Oxford University Press. There, the staff have all been most helpful, and particular thanks must go to the two anonymous reviewers who suggested numerous improvements and led me to a number of references that I had overlooked.

Finally, I would like to thank Dr Philip Gundry, of Imperial College, University of London, for his critical reading of the type-script and for suggesting a number of improvements that I was glad to adopt. The responsibility for any remaining errors is, of course, mine.

T. H. O'Dell

London
March 1994

1

Introduction

The combination of the two words 'secret' and 'patent' seems, at first sight, to be a contradiction. Secret means kept private, whereas *litterae patentes*, from where the English word 'patent' comes, are open letters from the sovereign conferring some right or privilege. And the letter is open, for everyone to read, so that everyone knows just what it is the sovereign has given away, and just what it was the subject had asked for. In the case of letters patent for an invention, the bargain between the sovereign (the state) and the subject (the inventor) is that the inventor gives a full description of the invention, which is then published, and, in exchange for this contribution to public knowledge, the state undertakes to grant the inventor a temporary monopoly so that the invention can be exploited, initially, entirely to the inventor's advantage.

There are, however, exceptions. Today any resident of the United Kingdom who applies for a patent to protect an invention may be told that the publication of the specification is prohibited. More than that, the publication, even the communication, of the *idea* described in the specification is prohibited. The penalties for ignoring this prohibition, or trying to get around it, can be severe. Patent applications that run into difficulties of this kind usually involve weapons, but the law is wide in its application. Section 22 of the 1977 Patents Act extended the powers of prohibiting publication to anything 'prejudicial to public safety'.

This book attempts to give the history of how 'secret patent' legislation developed in the United Kingdom. Its origins are surprisingly early in that the first case of prohibition to be found in the records occurred in 1855. The first Act of Parliament that specifically dealt with secret patents received royal assent in 1859. In tracing the thread of secret patents through the fabric of the history of inventions, patent law, and society in general, we come up against some interesting ideas and unusual people. Naturally, inventions that the state believed should be kept secret must have appeared important at the time. But what was happening at the time may well have been the reason for that. Indeed, what was happening at the time may well have been the reason for the invention in the first place.

The attempt to combine the history of inventions with social, economic, and patent law history is undoubtedly an ambitious and difficult task. It has been carried out with considerable success by Dutton (1984) in *The Patent System and Inventive Activity during the Industrial Revolution 1750–1852*, and by MacLeod (1988) in *Inventing the Industrial Revolution: The English Patent System 1660–1800*. This book is concerned with a later period. It was in 1852 that the first major Act of Parliament concerning patents for inventions was passed, and it was this Act that set up the Patent Office.

It was under the Act of 1852 that the first case of the British government prohibiting the publication of a patent specification occurred. This was in 1855, and the case is considered in Chapter 2, along with the events leading up to the 1852 Act. The secret patent became firmly established a few years later when the Act of 1859, dealt with in Chapter 3, laid down the rules for secret patents that were to remain virtually unchanged for the next ninety years. Towards the end of the nineteenth century the government felt that the need to make and keep secrets justified the first Official Secrets Act of 1889. This, along with the important Patents, Designs and Trade Marks Act of 1883, is the subject of Chapter 4. The late nineteenth century is particularly interesting in respect of its secrets because there is evidence that the manufacture of armaments at the time was undertaken in a surprisingly open way in the United Kingdom. Real know-how was thought to be unimportant, perhaps, while paper secrets were carefully guarded. This possibility is further suggested by the story told in Chapter 5 about Marconi and the Wright brothers. These inventors offered some secret know-how to the British government and got little response.

The beginning of the twentieth century saw the Patent Office getting down to the task of examining the technical content of patent applications, and thus weeding out applications that described ideas already claimed in earlier specifications. The Patent Office then had a full knowledge of the technical details of new inventions when the applications were still strictly confidential, and this precipitated some bitter exchanges between the Patent Office and the War Office. The Patent Office maintained its rules of confidentiality with great dignity. These battles are described in Chapter 6, which also covers the First World War. Chapter 7 deals with the time between the two world wars, when there were no important changes in the patent law in the United Kingdom but great changes in nearly everything else. The Official Secrets Act of 1920 arrived, to be used as another weapon to attack the confidential rules at the Patent Office, which fought this off with great skill. Three cases of secret patents are reviewed in the chapter, one being the well-known case involving Leo Szilard and the atomic bomb. Two secrets of the Second World War are looked at in Chapter 8: radar and the so-called dambuster bomb. It would be difficult to find two inventions of greater contrast. The Second World War was a time of intense technical activity and also a period particularly rich in records. This is also true of the years just after the war, when two important changes in the law concerning secrets took place: an Atomic Energy Act, in 1946, and a very important Patents Act in 1949. These are considered in Chapter 9 and lead to our last example of an invention that ran into secret patent difficulties: the hovercraft.

The final chapter attempts to draw some conclusions and find some reasons for the secrecy that has been an obsession of the British government for so long. An interesting event that illustrates this occurred in 1977, when the House of Lords voted, by a good majority, to abolish all the secrecy that had surrounded British patent law for well over a century. The House of Commons promptly put all the secrecy clauses back into the new 1977 Patents Bill, and made things a little more secret than they had been before. The Copyright, Designs and Patents Act of 1988, the most recent Act of Parliament to be mentioned in this book, made no changes whatsoever to the secret patent aspect of British patent law. It seems clear that we in the United Kingdom live in a highly secretive society, and the secret patent system is a product of this society. Other countries may well have secret patent systems of their own, but the British can surely claim that no other society had and used a secret patent system as early as 1855, and that their system has continued, and developed, up to the present day. In the next chapter, let us go back to 1855 and look at the case of the very first secret patent.

2

The First Secret Patent

2.1 John Macintosh

On 6 August 1855 one John Macintosh left a provisional specification at the Patent Office in London entitled 'Certain Improvements in the Application of Incendiary Materials to be Used in
Warfare'. This was not the first time that Macintosh had applied
for a patent. In fact, it was the fourth time that year, his previous
ideas for 1855 being in the more peaceful fields of pens, springs,
and matches. His application on 6 August is of particular interest
for this book, however, because it became what may be the first
example of the British government suppressing the publication of
a patent specification.

Under the new Patent Law Amendment Act of 1852 an inventor
was allowed a period of up to six months in which to perfect the
idea outlined in the provisional specification. At any time before
the six months expired a complete specification could be left at
the Patent Office and the inventor could then declare an intention
to proceed with his application for a patent. This 'Notice to Proceed' would then be published in the *Commissioners of Patents'
Journal*, giving the full title of the patent specification and the
inventor's name. Under section 12 of the 1852 Act, anyone could
now object to the application by writing to the commissioners. For
example, an employer, a master, as he would expect to be called,
might well object if he found one of his employees, one of his
men, trying to take out a patent on some aspect of the master's
manufacturing technique. Another inventor might well object when
he noticed a colleague attempting to patent an invention he had
trustingly thought they were planning to patent together. It must
be remembered that no details of the specification were public
knowledge at this confidential initial stage. Only the name of the
inventor and the title of the specification were published. It follows

that only people who had an intimate knowledge of the inventor and his field of work should have been in a position to object to his making an application for a patent. The Act of 1852, however, left the grounds for objection completely open.

John Macintosh wasted no time in announcing his intention to proceed with his incendiary patent application. This was published on 24 August 1855 (*CPJ* 172 at 311), only one week after the *Journal* had announced his application for provisional protection (*CPJ* 171 at 306). This was normal for Macintosh. His three other applications in 1855, in June, September, and October, all went through rapidly and were sealed, that is, a patent was actually issued, in November 1855. The August application was different: it was not sealed until 19 December 1856 (*CPJ* 309 at 1328).

2.2 Patent No. 1774 of 1855

Once a patent was sealed under the Act of 1852, the inventor had the title to the intellectual property, and the public, after the short delay needed for printing, would be able to buy a printed copy of the specification. Copies were also put into the library of the Patent Office, and many other public libraries where, with luck, they may be found today. When we look at Macintosh's incendiary patent (BPN 1774 of 1855), it is clear that it became a very special one. The first two pages of the specification are reproduced in Fig. 1. There are several unique features about the printed specification of British Patent No. 1774 of 1855. First, it has 'Second Edition' printed at the top of the first page. Secondly, we read that it has been sealed 'by Order of the Lord Chancellor'. All that the Act of 1852 required was a warrant from the Solicitor-General or the Attorney-General. Thirdly, after the provisional specification reference is again made to the Lord Chancellor's 'Order'. It is also odd that, although the patent was sealed on 19 December 1856, the specification does not seem to have been written until 10 January 1857, and the printed version that we see today, bearing the news of all these unusual happenings, would not have been available for some time after that.

A close observer of what was going on in the Lord Chancellor's court in 1856 would, however, have already heard most of the story. On 22 November 1856 Macintosh presented a petition, asking to have his patent No. 1774 sealed. During the hearing it

[Second Edition.]

A.D. 1855 . . . . Nº 1774.

Application of Incendiary Materials to be used in Warfare.

LETTERS PATENT to John Macintosh, of Great Ormond Street, in the County of Middlesex, for the Invention of " CERTAIN IMPROVEMENTS IN THE APPLICATION OF INCENDIARY MATERIALS TO BE USED IN WARFARE."

Sealed the 19th December 1856, by Order of the Lord Chancellor, and dated the 6th August 1855.

PROVISIONAL SPECIFICATION left by the said John Macintosh at the Office of the Commissioners of Patents, with his Petition, on the 6th August 1855.

    I, JOHN MACINTOSH, of Great Ormond Street, in the County Middlesex, 5 do hereby declare the nature of the said Invention for " CERTAIN IMPROVEMENTS IN THE APPLICATION OF INCENDIARY MATERIALS TO BE USED IN WARFARE," to be as follows :—

    This Invention relates to coal-tar naphtha, alone or in combination with other materials, to be used as an agent in attack and defence ; and consists, 10 first, in the application of coal-tar naphtha as a destructive agent in submarine and other vessels ; such naphtha may be discharged from boats or vessels by pumps, cocks, hose, or valves, in or on the water, and ignited by potassium or other fuses. Second, in the application of coal-tar naphtha mixed with gunpowder, india-rubber, and fibrous materials introduced into

FIG. 1. First two pages of John Macintosh's patent specification, BPN 1774 of 1855

A.D. 1855.—N° 1774.

Macintosh's Impts. in the Application of Incendiary Materials in Warfare.

shells and other missiles; also in filling shells with coal-tar naphtha containing potassium, for igniting when used in water; and also in filling shells with coal-tar naphtha mixed with phosphorus and bisulphuret of carbon, with bursting powder sufficient to open the shells.

SPECIFICATION filed in pursuance of the conditions of the Letters Patent, 5
 and of the above Order, by the said John Macintosh in the Great Seal
 Patent Office on the 10th January 1857.

 TO ALL TO WHOM THESE PRESENTS SHALL COME, I, JOHN
MACINTOSH, of Great Ormond Street, in the County of Middlesex, send
greeting. 10
 WHEREAS Her most Excellent Majesty Queen Victoria, by Her Letters
Patent, bearing date the Sixth day of August, in the year of our Lord One
thousand eight hundred and fifty-five, in the nineteenth year of Her reign, did,
for Herself, Her heirs and successors, give and grant unto me, the said John
Macintosh, Her special licence that I, the said John Macintosh, my executors, 15
administrators, and assigns, or such others as I, the said John Macintosh, my
executors, administrators, and assigns, should at any time agree with, and no
others, from time to time and at all times thereafter during the term therein
expressed, should and lawfully might make, use, exercise, and vend, within
the United Kingdom of Great Britain and Ireland, the Channel Islands, and 20
Isle of Man, an Invention for "CERTAIN IMPROVEMENTS IN THE APPLICATION OF
INCENDIARY MATERIALS TO BE USED IN WARFARE," upon the condition (amongst
others) that I, the said John Macintosh, my executors or administrators, by
an instrument in writing under my, or their, or one of their hands and seals,
should particularly describe and ascertain the nature of the said Invention, and 25
in what manner the same was to be performed, and cause the same to be
filed in the Great Seal Patent Office on or before the Tenth day of Janary,
One thousand eight hundred and fifty-seven.
 NOW KNOW YE, that I, the said John Macintosh, do hereby declare the
nature of my said Invention, and in what manner the same is to be per- 30
formed, to be particularly described and ascertained in and by the following
statement:—
 My Invention consists in methods of facilitating attack on stronghold
batteries on shore, and on fleets, dockyards, harbours, towns, and other objects;
and in methods of defence against the approach of an enemy. When it is 35

emerged that the Solicitor-General had issued a warrant for sealing on 18 December 1855. Once this had been done, the complete
specification, now on its way to the printer, was public knowledge,
but not for long. Only a few hours must have passed that day
before the solicitor at the War Office issued an objection, under
section 12 of the 1852 Act. The text of his objection became widely
known only four years later, when the *Mechanics' Magazine* (25
March 1859, p. 198) published it as part of one of its regular tirades
against government restrictions on the freedom of inventors. It
ran as follows:

Patent Law Amendment Act, 1852.

I, Charles George Bannister, of Pall Mall, Middlesex, Solicitor for the
War Department, and for and on behalf of Her Majesty's Principal Secretary of State for the War Department, hereby give notice that I object
to the sealing of Letters Patent to John Macintosh, of Great Ormond
Street, Middlesex, for the Invention of 'Improvements in the application
of Incendiary Materials to be used in Warfare' as set forth in the warrant
of the Solicitor-General for the sealing of such Letters Patent, received
and recorded in the Office of the Commissioners of Patents for Inventions, on the 18th. Day of December, 1855. And my objections to the
sealing of such Letters Patent are as follows:—That such an invention can
only be useful in time of war, and that the publication of it may be
prejudicial to Her Majesty's service.

Dated this 18th. day of December, 1855.

(Signed) Chas G. Bannister,
Solicitor, War Department.

The digest of the court proceedings (*HPC* 11 at 287) makes it
clear that Macintosh had agreed, back in December 1855, to delay
going ahead with his patent application, and to co-operate fully
with whatever the Secretary of State for War required. What this
was precisely we shall never know, but the reason for all the fuss
is obvious. The Crimean War, which had started in October 1853,
had progressed through the winter of 1854–5 with the most terrible loss of life, and did not end until 30 March 1856. The number
of British soldiers killed in the fiasco was 45,000 (*EB* 11, 7 at 453).
In such circumstances, reading Macintosh's specification would have
been exciting to anyone. He proposed to spray the waters around
the fortified Russian ports of Kronstadt and Sevastopol with coal
tar, and then set the resulting mess ablaze by firing balls of potassium into it. He went on to claim that the burning coal tar would

generate 'a dense black suffocating fog or vapour, which envelopes the fort or battery, rushing into casements or embrasures and driving away the gunners and all engaged therein'. The specification continued with proposals for incendiary shells, or rockets with warheads, filled with a mixture of naphtha and potassium.

The digest of the court proceedings tells us that, although the Secretary of State relaxed his restrictions on Macintosh only a few weeks after the peace treaty was signed in Paris, on 30 March 1856, he still asked for, and Macintosh agreed to, a further delay in publication, and this continued until November 1856. Such a long delay meant that it was no longer possible, under the 1852 Act, for the patent to go ahead, and this was the reason for Macintosh's petition to the Lord Chancellor. The matter was not easily resolved. The Lord Chancellor's order was not made until 15 December 1856, when he decided that this was a special case 'within the equitable scope if not within the provisions' of the statute (*HPC* 7 at 288). Later still, in June 1860, a final piece of information became public knowledge that went a long way towards explaining why Macintosh had been so happy to co-operate with the Secretary of State for War: he had been given a research grant of £1,000 (serious money at that time). We know this from an interesting list giving 'the Amount of Public Money advanced since 1852 to Private Persons for the purpose of enabling them to make Experiments for . . . Improving WEAPONS of WAR' (BPP 1860 (386), xli. 639). The list includes many famous names: Armstrong, Krupp, Nasmyth, and Whitworth, among a total of twenty-eight people who, in all, received nearly £73,000 over the eight years.

The story about John Macintosh's incendiary fantasies and his good luck in getting both a research grant and a patent out of the British government is our starting-point for a longer story concerned with inventors, the Patent Office, and what we would call today the Ministry of Defence. Let us begin by taking a look at the origins of the Patent Law Amendment Act of 1852 which seems to have served Macintosh so well. These origins lie in the old law that governed patents for inventions before 1852.

2.3 The Old Law

The most important point about the old law was that the granting of a patent for an invention was entirely a matter of royal prerogative. The Statute of Monopolies of 1623 had made the granting of all monopolies illegal, except those for the 'sole working or making of any manner of new manufacture within the realm to the true and first inventor of such manufacture, which others at the time of making such letters patent should not use, so they be not contrary to law' (*EB* 11, 20 at 903). To obtain such a patent, an inventor, or rather the person who claimed to be the first inventor, had to give a full description of the invention and make an application through many officials, in many different offices, for the documents that had to be prepared. These documents were then presented, with a positive recommendation, for the sovereign to sign. The resulting patent could then be used to prevent other people from using the invention, or it could be used to get other people to pay a royalty. Under the old law, a patent could be overturned only if it could be proved in court that the description given in the patent was either incomplete or too wide in its claims, if it was wrong in any detail, or if the idea had been published somewhere else at an earlier date.

Under the old law, patents were too expensive, too easily used for fraud, and too easily obtained for ideas that were not new. On the question of expense, Charles Dickens wrote an amusing short story, 'The Poor Man's Tale of a Patent'. This was published in 1850 (Phillips (1984)) and tells of how John, the hero of the tale, is relieved of £96. 7s. 8*d*. as he trudges from one office to another preparing his application for a patent. At the end John asks, 'Is it reasonable to make a man feel as if, in inventing an ingenious improvement meant to do good, he had done something wrong?'

Dutton's (1984) interesting book on the patent system in the United Kingdom, covering the years between 1750 and 1852, gives a vivid picture of the agitation, which came from both inventors and manufacturers early in the nineteenth century, for radical reform of the patent law. One important centre of propaganda for reform was a house in Chancery Lane, where the London Mechanics' Institute had its headquarters. Founded by the philanthropist George Birkbeck (1776–1841) and the utopian socialist Thomas Hodgskin (1787–1869), this institute, later to become Birkbeck College of the University of London, published the widely read *Mechanics' Magazine*, which was specifically intended to serve the needs of inventors by giving some details of what the new patents described. The magazine agitated for patent law reform and reported any patent matters that came up in Parliament.

There were, on the other hand, strong conservative voices raised against patent law reform. It is not at all clear what precipitated the setting up of a select committee of the House of Commons, in 1829, to look into the question. At the time, the agitation for reform from inventors and manufacturers was particularly weak. Protest meetings called for by the London Mechanics' Institute were poorly attended (Dutton (1984), 43), and the editor of the *Mechanics' Magazine* was in the process of setting himself up as a patent agent (Van Zyl Smit (1985), 91).

2.4   The 1829 Select Committee

The instigator of the 1829 select committee was Thomas B. Lennard (1788–1856), MP for Maldon in Essex. He was an 'advanced but independent Whig' who, in 1820, had spent £12,000 to get his first seat in the Commons (Barrett-Lennard (1908), 637). There was no particular reason for Lennard to be interested in patent law reform. His notebooks of the time (ERO: D/DL O48/1–4) show that he was interested in reform of all kinds: electoral reform, tax reform, the abolition of capital punishment for robbery, and so on. He was a man of immense wealth and could easily afford his Liberal outlook. Lennard spoke in the Commons on 9 April 1829, moving 'that a select committee be appointed to inquire into the present state of the Law and Practice relative to the granting of Letters-patent for Inventions' (H2, 21 at 606). There was no opposition to the idea and a committee was appointed, Lennard being chairman. One member was Sir Robert Peel, Secretary of State for Home Affairs in the Tory government of the Duke of Wellington which was in power at the time.

The select committee met for the first time on 11 May, when the first witness was the engineer John Farey. Secrecy was soon being discussed:

'In France, are not secret patents taken out?'
'In France, the specifications are always kept secret during the term of the patent, and even afterwards when the government decide that it is advisable to do so. The specification has sometimes been kept secret in this country, by express Act of Parliament'.

Farey did not give any examples of such early 'secret patents'. What he was referring to were cases where the inventor had asked for secrecy for commercial reasons, and there had been two Acts during the long reign of George III that had made such secret patents (Dutton (1984), 42 n. 45). This was certainly something that patent law reformers would have hoped to make impossible.

The select committee's second witness was Marc Isambard Brunel (1769–1849), the father of the equally great engineer Isambard Kingdom Brunel (1806–59). During his evidence we find the modern concept of a secret patent being discussed, perhaps for the first time:

'What would be your opinion of giving power to the Secretary of State or some other authority, to direct the specification to be concealed in certain cases?'

'I do not know what is the motive for concealing it; if it is on behalf of the inventor, that is some reason, but if it is to prevent its going abroad it is of no use, because if it is good it will soon make its way, and if it is not it is of no consequence.'

Such a firm grasp of reality comes across during all of the elder Brunel's interrogation. The committee came back to a point Lennard had raised in the Commons when he said: 'It was a sort of proverb among inventors, that he who took out a patent [under the old law] took out a law suit with it', and that a patent really had no value until it had gone through with this law suit and had been 'confirmed by the verdict of a jury' (H2, 21 at 601). The elder Brunel agreed: 'I have frequently said, that I might as well toss [a coin] for the fate of a patent; it is an intricate question for a jury, and in many cases it is quite unintelligible to them.'

This kind of lively criticism did not persist, however. After the two engineers, Farey and Brunel, the committee saw mainly patent agents. Moses Poole, for example, a clerk in the Attorney-General's office, and whom Van Zyl Smit (1985) considers to be one of the founding fathers of the profession of patent agents, told the committee that there was little wrong with the patent law as it stood. The only problem, as far as he was concerned, was that the King, George IV, had to sign the final papers, which could be a problem, Poole explained, 'when he is not well'. George IV was often unwell.

The report, minutes of evidence taken, and documents received by the select committee were all published on 12 June 1829 (BPP 1829 (332), iii. 415). The report was brief and explained that the subject of the inquiry was 'in its nature so intricate and important' that they would ask the House to allow them to resume next session. In the event, Lennard's select committee never met again. He tried, with some other MPs, to get a bill through Parliament in 1833, but this got nowhere. Lord Brougham managed to get a short 'Act to amend the Law touching Letters Patent for Invention' through in 1835 (5 & 6 Will. IV, c. 83), which removed the problems inventors ran into when one small part of the claims they might have made in their specifications proved to be invalid. When this happened, under the old law, the whole patent collapsed. Apart from this modest revision, there were no other changes in the patent law after the 1829 select committee submitted its evidence until 1852.

The reason for this lack of interest on the part of the government for over twenty years is not hard to understand: they had more pressing problems to consider than patent law reform. In 1830 the Tory monopoly of power, which had held sway for the early years of the nineteenth century, collapsed. Earl Grey's Whig party took over, and radical reform of the entire constitution of the United Kingdom was attempted.

The reform in the electoral laws,which took place in 1832, certainly made a beginning at the task of preventing bribery and corruption in elections, and enfranchised many middle-class citizens, while still excluding the working class. Evidence that things were still rather undemocratic has been left for us by Charles Dickens who, writing in 1836–7, gave a vivid picture of the drunken chaos that could take place at election time (Dickens (1986), 236–55). It must be remembered that there was no secret ballot in England until 1872.

2.5 The Great Exhibition

Patent law reform was taken up again during the Whig administration of Lord John Russell, which held power from 1846 to 1852. The reason was that a Great Exhibition was to be held in London in 1851, the Exhibition of the Works of Industry of All Nations. This came up in the House of Commons on 1 April 1851, when a short discussion of the problem of patent law reform took place

(H3, 115 at 890–5). The discussion started in a rather strange manner when an MP, one Colonel Sibthorp, began a confused speech about patents costing far too much, and then launched into a chauvinistic tirade against the very idea of the Great Exhibition. He was reported as saying:

all kinds of foreigners were to come here, talking all kinds of gibberish . . . the English people would not understand them, and they [the foreigners] would get into all kinds of disturbances . . . and pirate the inventions of our countrymen . . . take them home, make up the same manufactures at a cheaper rate, and then send them here and undersell the ingenious and laborious mechanics of our own land.

Perhaps the Colonel had been set up as April Fool of the House for 1851. After a few MPs had expressed surprise, or regret, at what the Colonel had said, the President of the Board of Trade closed the discussion by telling the House that Lord Granville, his vice-president, would be introducing a bill for patent law reform within a few days.

In fact there were two bills. One had been framed by Lord Brougham (1778–1868), who, at this stage in his remarkable career, had no position in the government but prepared bills on a wide variety of things. The second bill had been framed by Lord Granville (1815–91), who was vice-president of the Board of Trade in Lord John Russell's Whig administration. A select committee of the House of Lords was appointed on 11 April 1851 to consider the two bills, and it started work on 15 April, under the chairmanship of Lord Granville. Lord Granville's attitude towards patents becomes clear from a reading of the debate that took place in the House of Lords (H3, 118 at 5–18) on 1 July 1851, a few days before the report of the select committee was published. He mentioned that some of the witnesses who were called before the committee had 'maintained that there was an absolute innate right of property in ideas'. He himself did not want to go into 'any absolute question [concerning] property in intellectual objects, [but] he would contend that it was impossible to define property in an idea'. As the debate continued it became clear that Lord Granville tended strongly towards the idea of complete abolition of the patent system. This was a proposal that was to find widespread support within a few years, and which will be dealt with at length in Chapter 3. Lord Granville continued in the debate to make it clear that he believed neither in intellectual property, nor in the idea that the patent system acted as an incentive for invention. He concluded that 'the only persons ... who derive any advantage from the patent laws, were members of the legal profession', but, nevertheless, he understood that the majority of people at that time wanted such a law, and Parliament had to decide how to turn the existing bad law into at least a better one.

2.6 The 1851 Select Committee

In view of their chairman's convictions, it is hardly surprising that the report of the select committee of 1851, which was published on 4 July (BPP 1851 (486), xviii. 255), contrasts somewhat with the comfortable tone of Lennard's 1829 report. For example, where Lennard had the elder Brunel as one of his witnesses, Lord Granville called the younger, Isambard Kingdom Brunel, who remarked:

I have never taken out a patent myself, or ever thought of taking one, or, I hope, ever shall take one; and certainly from the experience I have had, and all that I have seen of the operation of patents, I believe them to be productive of almost unmixed evil with respect to every party connected with them, whether those for the benefit of whom they are apparently made, or the public.

And the younger Brunel was not alone in holding such revolutionary opinions. Charles May, a manufacturer, told the 1851 committee, 'I think the class of inventors are certainly the creation of the patent law.' J. H. Lloyd, a barrister, was for abolition and expressed the free trade concept in intellectual property clearly when he said that real talent would always find its market value. The index of the report listed seven of the thirty-five witnesses in favour of abolition, and this did not include the chairman or the MP J. L. Ricardo, whose evidence was given in an appendix. J. L. Ricardo (1812–62), nephew of David Ricardo (1772–1823), came to be best remembered for the time when he rode one of his horses up the staircase of his great country house, and then on into the dining-room (Lee (1896)). He was MP for Stoke-on-Trent at the time of Lord Granville's inquiry, and he was a 'free trader'.

The free traders were a relatively new political party, and they represented the interests of the great manufacturers. Led by

Richard Cobden (1804–65) and John Bright (1811–89), they were bitterly opposed to any kind of regulation. Cobden, for example, is mentioned in Gomme's short history of the patent system in the UK as being in favour of the complete abolition of patents (Gomme (1946), 42).

On 21 July 1851 the two new patent bills, Lord Brougham's and Lord Granville's, combined by the 1851 select committee and now polished by the House of Lords, were presented to the Commons. A lively debate took place (H3, 118 at 1534–48). J. L. Ricardo was of the opinion that 'the whole system was an abomination which should be done away with', and this remark provoked a violent counter-attack from Roundell Palmer, an MP of only a few years' standing, who had spent ten years as a barrister in the Court of Chancery and was now at the start of the brilliant political career that was to make him Lord Chancellor in 1872. We shall be hearing more of Roundell Palmer in this book, because he was to have his views on patents radically altered by experience.

With such extreme views being expressed in the House of Commons, it is perhaps not surprising that the new bill, which had fifty-four clauses, was still being debated up to the day that Parliament was prorogued, 7 August 1851. Prorogation meant that the bill was lost, and work would have to start from scratch when Parliament met again. This did not happen until February 1852.

2.7   A Change of Government

There were good political reasons for Parliament standing prorogued from August 1851 to February 1852, which were far removed from the field of patent law reform. Virtual panic had swept the United Kingdom as a result of the re-establishment of the French Empire under Louis Napoleon: invasion, the press warned, was imminent. Lord John Russell could not cope with the situation and, when Parliament did at last meet again, remained Prime Minister only from 3 February until 23 February, when he resigned. During those action-filled days, Lord Brougham, now nearly 74 years old, managed to introduce yet another of his bills for patent law reform, on 13 February, but as he did it 'in a scarcely audible voice' (H3, 119 at 495) it can be put aside.

Queen Victoria had sent for the Earl of Derby (1799–1869) to form a new, Tory, government, and, in view of the subject being

considered in this book, it is interesting to quote from his first
speech as the new Prime Minister, because he mentioned what
today we would call state security. Considering the situation in
Europe at the time, it is not surprising that he did. He reminded
their lordships that, under the institutions of the United Kingdom,
which the new government intended to conserve:

we are not only free and tranquil at home, but we are, as we have always
been—and God forbid that we should ever cease to be!—an ark of refuge
for those whose misfortunes have driven them as exiles from their own
homes to seek protection here ... [and who] ... find here safe and tranquil asylum. [But the government has a duty] to keep guard over the
conduct of such persons as are disposed to abuse our hospitality ... without
descending to a system—I must use a French word for it, for, thank God,
we have not an English one which expresses it—of *espionage* or *surveillance*, which is adverse to all the feelings of the country (H3, 119 at 896).

2.8 The Act of 1852

In the new atmosphere of conserving the United Kingdom's institutions, patent law reform could go ahead at full speed. The bill
that had been under consideration in 1851 had proposed a staff of
examiners, state officials who would read the applications for
patents and see if the ideas put forward were both new and useful.
The 1852 Parliament thought that it interfered with the royal prerogative and, perhaps even worse, cost money (H3, 121 at 1221–
34). Out with the examiners. The 1851 bill had proposed that
ideas that were well known abroad should not be patentable in
the United Kingdom. On that idea, G. F. Muntz, arms manufacturer and MP for Birmingham, contributed to the debate by saying that one could 'get foreigners to swear anything'. So, out with
that idea too. But the most effective destruction of the previous
Parliament's work on patent law reform came from the future
Lord Chancellor Roundell Palmer. He saw 'the hand of Lord
Granville' in all this, who, 'with great candour ... had stated in
another place, that he was unfriendly to the whole principle of
patent law, and that he looked forward to its entire abolition'.

After a great deal of work in both Houses of Parliament, the
bill received royal assent on 1 July 1852 (15 & 16 Vict., c. 83). All
that was left of the previous year's plans for patent law reform was
the idea to create a centralized patent office, with a library and

funds to publish not only all future specifications but all the old ones as well. This took a long time to realize. An attempt was made to accommodate the new Patent Office and its library in a few rooms within one of the old buildings off the north-east end of Chancery Lane, and it was not until 1895 that these were demolished and the new Patent Office and library could be built. Section 16 of the 1852 Act made it clear that nothing in the new Act was to affect the prerogative of the Crown in granting or withholding patents. The old rules still applied: if an inventor was granted a patent, it was up to an offended party to bring a case in the Court of Chancery to show why the patent should not have been granted.

There were a few positive points in the new law. The cost of obtaining a patent was reduced: the fees now went directly to the Solicitor-General and the Attorney-General. Previously, there had been numerous officials and petty clerks who demanded fees individually. Another good reform was that a patent granted in London was valid over the whole of the United Kingdom of Great Britain and Ireland. Previously, England and Wales, Scotland, and Ireland had each required a separate patent.

And, finally, section 12 of the 1852 Act was the one used by the Secretary of State for War to suppress the publication of John Macintosh's fantastic plans to set the sea ablaze. Surely it had not been the intention of the government that section 12 would be used as an instrument of surveillance, the very idea of which the Earl of Derby had assured Parliament was 'adverse to all the feelings of the country'.

3

The Secret Patents Act of 1859

3.1 Munitions of War

On 21 March 1859 Sir Fitzroy Kelly (1796–1880), Attorney-General in the Earl of Derby's second Tory administration, introduced the Patents for Inventions (Munitions of War) Bill to the House of Commons (H3, 153 at 482). The bill, he explained, was 'intended to accomplish a very important object', in that 'it was thought that inventions respecting munitions of war, or others of a character which it was for the public interest to conceal, should be vested in the Crown'. He went on to describe the procedures that were proposed for 'sealing up' and 'keeping secret' the specifications of these patents, and concluded that 'to such a proposal there could . . . be no objections because, in ancient times it was the prerogative of the Crown to secure to itself an exclusive right to all inventions of a military character. The Bill was therefore only in furtherance of the ancient common law.' Parliament clearly accepted this. The bill received royal assent in less than three weeks, on 8 April 1859. There was no discussion, no amendment, and no debate, thus giving today's reader no clue as to the origin of the bill or the reason for such haste. Perhaps the British government had either just lost a good secret or had just got hold of one. It is interesting to enquire what the secret might have been.

The *Mechanics' Magazine* was incensed about the proposed bill. Writing one week before it received royal assent, the editor spoke for 'England' as follows: 'We are beyond all question both the richest and the ablest people on the face of the earth, and no devices of secrecy are needed in order to keep us in our proper position' (1 April 1859, p. 213).

But again this was the propaganda of the Whigs and free traders saying, 'Away with regulation', while at the same time, as we saw in Section 2.3, the *Mechanics' Magazine* editor, the propagandist Robertson, was in the process of setting himself up as a patent agent. Similarly, Sir Fitzroy Kelly's appeal to 'ancient common law', and his respect for the 'prerogative of the Crown', were typical of early-nineteenth-century Tory doublethink—a phenomenon commented upon by an outstanding Tory of the time, Benjamin Disraeli. He had the principal character in his 1844 novel *Coningsby* explain:

Thus they are devoted to the prerogative of the Crown, although in truth the Crown has been stripped of every one of its prerogatives; they affect a great veneration for the constitution in Church and State, though everyone knows that the constitution in Church and State no longer exists; they are ready to stand or fall with the independence of the Upper House of Parliament, though, in practice, they are perfectly aware that, with their sanction, the Upper House has abdicated its initiatory functions, and now serves only as a court of review of the legislation of the House of Commons. Whenever public opinion, which this party never attempts to form, to educate, or to lead, falls into some violent perplexity, passion or caprice, this party yields without struggle to the impulse, and, when the storm has passed, attempts to obstruct and obviate the logical and, ultimately, the inevitable results of the very measures they themselves originated, or to which they have consented. This is the Conservative party (Disraeli (1989), 372).

3.2   William Armstrong

Let us return to the question of why the British government introduced the 1859 bill, and were in such unseemly haste to get it through Parliament. A clue that William Armstrong (1810–1900), the weapons manufacturer, might have been involved comes from two facts: a few weeks before the bill was introduced, he was appointed engineer for rifled ordnance to the British government, at a salary of £2,000 per annum, backdated for three years (BPP 1862 (448), vi. 111), and at the same time he became Sir William Armstrong. That Armstrong was the cause of the 1859 bill being framed is clear from the *Report of the Commissioners Appointed to Inquire into the Working of the Law relating to Letters Patent for Inventions*, which was printed on 29 July 1864 (BPP 1864 (3419), xxix. 321–576). The report will be considered in detail below, but the important witness for the question of the moment was C. M. Clode, solicitor to the War Office.

Clode was asked how useful the Patents for Inventions (Munitions of War) Act of 1859 (22 Vict., c. 13) had been to his department. He replied that the bill had been 'framed when Sir William

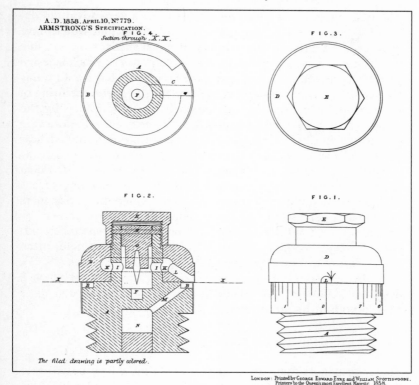

A.D. 1858. APRIL 10, N° 779.
ARMSTRONG'S SPECIFICATION.

LONDON: Printed by GEORGE EDWARD EYRE and WILLIAM SPOTTISWOODE, Printers to the Queen's most Excellent Majesty. 1858.

FIG. 2. Drawings from William Armstrong's patent specification, BPN 779 of 1858

Armstrong's invention first came out', and in later written evidence he made it clear which one of Armstrong's many inventions he referred to, and also what the problem had been:

In 1858 (and the same practice may still exist), it was the practice of our Patent Office to send specifications of English inventions, as soon as they were published, to Paris, Berlin, etc., and it was ascertained that Sir W. Armstrong, by patenting his time and percussion fuze in April, 1858, had, by doing so, given it (by making it known) to foreign powers, although his own Sovereign could not use it till he subsequently assigned it to the Secretary for War.

Certainly, Armstrong's 1858 patent (BPN 779 of 1858) is a complete specification, with the most detailed drawings (see Fig. 2).

The patent described what was, for its time, a very advanced design for a time-and-percussion fuse of the kind that would have been used on large-calibre artillery or naval shells. How sensible was it—indeed, how sensible is it—to attempt to keep such a design secret? Armstrong's design may have involved what would today be called an 'inventive step', in that the time between the firing of the gun and the explosion of the shell was determined by the setting of an annular scale. This scale may be seen in the drawing on the lower right of Fig. 2. The scale setting determined how much of the annular channel (marked B in the two left-hand drawings) had to burn before ignition reached the channel M, which then burnt down to fire the main detonator, N. Keeping such a design secret would have little effect upon competitive designers of time-and-percussion fuses. As many authors have shown, by careful research of the records, the same idea can come independently to many workers in one technical or scientific field, often within the same week (Merton (1973); Ogburn and Thomas (1922)). It is also arguable that a better idea may be put aside when a designer is influenced by outside knowledge, which has been made over-important by an attempt to keep it secret.

3.3   The Commissioner's Report of 1864

The chairman of the 1864 commission appointed to inquire into the working of the patent law was Lord Stanley (1826–93). He was MP for King's Lynn until 1869, when his father died and he became the fifteenth Earl of Derby, taking his seat in the House of Lords. He was a man of remarkable ability, becoming Foreign Secretary when his father took over as Prime Minister, for the third time, in 1866. From the beginning of his political career, he was a most liberal Conservative, and he became a member of Gladstone's second Liberal administration in 1882.

Over twenty witnesses were called before Lord Stanley's commission, and the report of their evidence, supplemented by a number of appendices, covers over 250 pages. The report itself, which detailed the commissioner's conclusions, proposed only minor changes in the existing patent law, because 'the inconveniences now generally complained of by the public as incident to the working of the patent law . . . cannot be wholly removed . . . and must be considered as the price which the public consents to pay for the existence of such law'. A conclusion so mild was only to be expected in view of the wide spectrum of opinion that was coming as evidence from the witnesses. For example, Sir William Armstrong was called as a witness. He first admitted that if he could have his way he would abolish all patents but, realizing that it was a minority opinion at the time, he would say no more. He went on to explain some of the difficulties patent law ran into when trying to deal with cases of multiple invention or inventions that were simply obvious adaptations of well-known ideas. He also stated that he believed there was no truth in the idea that the prospect of a patent acted as an incentive to invent, a point that will be taken up at the end of this book. In Armstrong's evidence we find one of the earliest expositions of the idea that invention and innovation are distinct. He made it clear that he thought inventing something new was not the difficult step: the problem was working out a good, manufacturable, design for a new idea, getting it made, and then getting people to buy it. As Kingston has put it: 'To invent is to find a new thing, to innovate is to get a new thing done' (Kingston (1984), 1).

Armstrong's industry, his whole life in fact, was devoted to armaments (Dougan (1970), McKenzie (1983)). Despite this, there was no mention, during his examination before the 1864 Royal Commission, of munitions or secrecy problems. In contrast, the commissioners were brought face to face with such matters when the twelfth Duke of Somerset (1804–85) was called as a witness. He was at the time First Lord of the Admiralty, and a politician of great experience, having served as an MP for a number of boroughs for the twenty-five years prior to his succession in 1855.

The Duke had brought one of his admirals along with him, and they began by explaining to the commissioners the 'great inconvenience' the Admiralty suffered from 'the present state of the law'. For example, the Duke explained, the Admiralty had bought the patent rights of one Robert Griffiths in 1859 which covered the design of a variable-pitch propeller (BPN 319 of 1859), and the records (PRO: TS21/44) show that Griffiths received a royalty of 2s. 6d. for each horsepower of installed engines needed to drive his propellers: such an arrangement would have provided him with a considerable fortune. The Duke, however, went on to say that this had all turned sour because 'I had repeated letters from Sir Howard Douglas . . . that he had invented all this'. Douglas was an outstanding military engineer, but he was over 83 when he wrote repeatedly to the Duke, an age when even the most distinguished men may come to believe that they have invented nearly everything. The important point, however, is that Douglas knew what the Admiralty's arrangements were. It is clear that they must have been fairly open about things.

Further evidence for the lack of secrecy in defence matters in the mid-nineteenth century came from another witness before the 1864 commissioners, General J. H. Lefroy. The general's evidence made it clear that the War Office had considerable respect for intellectual property rights. Even experiments would be delayed until they knew what rights patentees might have. How did the patentees know what the War Office might have been experimenting with? The answer was very simple: the patentees were in the service of the Crown. There were no restrictions at the time on members of the armed services applying for patents.

Finally, the evidence of the War Office solicitor, C. M. Clode, must be looked at again. We saw above, in Section 3.2, that his evidence was the key to the 1859 Act, and the part played by Armstrong in the framing of the Act. What did Clode have to say about the Act itself? It is clear from the evidence that he thought that the Patents for Inventions (Munitions of War) Act of 1859 was a rather ineffective instrument as far as the War Office was concerned. The problem was that the patent had to be acquired, in its provisional form, before the complete specification could be 'kept secret' and 'sealed up'. If the patentee did not agree to sell the patent, there was nothing much the Crown could do under the 1859 Act. The problem was not to be solved for a long time; it will be taken up again in Chapter 4.

The effects of the 1859 Act may be seen today, however, when we look at the printed specifications of these old patents, the ones published after 1859 and up to 1883, when the law was changed. For example, Armstrong's patents on rifled ordnance (BPN 611 of 1859) and on breech-loading (BPN 743 of 1861) are both cases where the patents were acquired by the Crown in the provisional form, and the complete specifications then kept secret. In contrast to Armstrong's 1858 patent, with its detailed drawings (see Fig. 2), the 1859 and 1861 patents consist of less than a single page of text, just giving an outline of the subject, and there are no diagrams or actual design details. That this means we may be looking at a secret patent is confirmed by Gomme in his short history of the patent system in the United Kingdom. For once he drops his guard in not giving away any administrative secrets of the British Patent Office, and tells us the important fact that 'provisional specifications that were not followed by a complete specification were also printed up to the year 1883, but since that year *have not been published or accessible to the public*' (Gomme (1946), 36–7; emphasis added).

3.4 The Abolitionists

On 28 May 1869 R. A. Macfie (1811–93), MP for the Burgh of Leith, Edinburgh, introduced a motion in the House of Commons proposing the complete abolition of the patent system. The possibility that this could happen was, clearly, accepted by *The Times*. A leading article in the issue of 29 May 1869 confirmed that the movement for the abolition of patents had made great progress in Europe recently. The Netherlands had abolished their system of patent law, first established in 1817 when Belgium and the Netherlands were still united. It was not to be restored until 1912. Switzerland had no patent system at the time, and Prussia, which had introduced a patent system in 1815, would have abolished it in 1868 if the wishes of Chancellor Otto von Bismarck had been followed (BPP 1870 (41), lxi. 527). *The Times* confidently predicted the imminent abolition of the British patent system, and a few days later, on 5 June, *The Economist* followed suit.

As Machlup and Penrose (1950) have observed in their study of the abolition movement, the whole story has been virtually forgotten today. The abolition movement throws some light on aspects of the history of secret patents, however, and the first event to be considered is the debate that Macfie started off in the House of Commons. Macfie was the owner of a major section of the sugar-refining industry, and he had retired from active business life at the age of 52 to devote himself to public work, both as an MP and as a prolific author of texts on the patent system and on religious matters. He opened the 1869 debate (H3, 196 at 888) on his motion 'That in the opinion of this House, the time has arrived when the interests of trade and commerce and the progress of the arts and sciences in this country would be promoted by the abolition of Patents for Inventions'. In speaking to his motion Macfie reviewed

the past select committees and commissions that had considered
the reform of the patent law, and reported on several meetings,
in both the United Kingdom and Europe, which had come to
the conclusion that patents should be abolished. He wanted a
new commission to be set up to settle the matter once and for
all.

Macfie's motion was seconded by Sir Roundell Palmer. This
must have been a surprise to some MPs who had heard him, back
in 1851, speaking as a strong supporter of the patent system (see
Section 2.6). In 1851 Roundell Palmer was reported to have said:
'The class who contributed by their ingenuity and their inventive
genius to the happiness of mankind were a special class, and they
would never apply their minds to the arts and sciences, but for the
assurance which they saw in the patent law of an eventual remuneration' (H3, 218 at 1544). Clearly, Sir Roundell Palmer had had
some experience of this 'special class' since 1851, because in 1869
he supported Macfie's abolition motion at length. His 'special class'
of 1851 were now applying their 'inventive genius' to such an
extent that 'the authorities at the War Office and the Admiralty
had patentees swarming like hornets about their ears' (H3, 196 at
900). And he concluded that 'the time had at last arrived—even if
it had not arrived some time ago—at which the public interest
would be promoted by the entire abolition of the present system
of monopoly' (H3, 196 at 903).

The man who had been the cause of Sir Roundell Palmer's
radical change of opinion on the patent question was one Robert
B. Feather, who described himself as a Liverpool merchant, and
who in 1852 had applied for a patent on the 'Construction of
Ships: Rendering Ships and Boats Impervious to Shot' (BPN 884
of 1852). The patent was granted and the complete specification,
which was published in May 1853, gave full details, with drawings,
of Feather's idea, which was to cover the hull of a wooden ship
with iron above the water-line only, and then to cover the protec-
tive iron plating with 'well prepared hides or sheets of . . . india
rubber'. There was, clearly, no great inventive step involved here,
and it is not known if Feather ever made any income, either from
making such ships or from royalties on his patent. One thing is
certain, however. In 1863, ten years after his patent was granted,
he applied to the Attorney-General for permission to file a disclaimer and amendment. This was allowed under the Act of 1852;

in fact, it was the same ruling set up by Lord Brougham's Act of 1835 (see Section 2.4).

The Attorney-General in 1863 was none other than Sir Roundell Palmer. This was his second appointment as a law officer in the Whig administration which ruled from 1859 to 1866. There was, of course, no reason for the Attorney-General not to give his fiat for the disclaimer that Feather wished to make, and this can be found today in the printed specifications, bound together with the 1852 patent and dated 2 November 1863. In a preamble Feather tells us that he has amended his original 1852 specification 'by striking out therefrom the words letters and figures, erased by red ink'. The last two pages of the amended disclaimer are reproduced in Fig. 3. These show that the printer chose to print the lines that Feather struck out and, as a printer's note tells us, print in italic what Feather had added in red ink. All this makes the printed specification unique. The closing paragraph, which, as always in a patent specification, summarizes the claims, shows that only the first claim remains. Roundell Palmer's fiat is printed at the very end. Feather disclaimed virtually everything in his 1852 patent except the idea of making a ship, in the conventional way, out of wood and then covering it with iron plates above the water-line. The reason he did this was that the Admiralty had just launched a ship, HMS *Enterprise*, which used precisely this composite structure.

Feather then brought a case for the infringement of his patent No. 884 against the Crown: the famous case of *Feather* v. *Regina* in 1865 (*HPC* 8 at 743–62). The defence for the Crown was conducted by the Attorney-General, Sir Roundell Palmer, who argued that the Crown had a prerogative to defend the realm and that no subject's patent rights could interfere with that prerogative. The Crown won the case on these grounds, and as we shall see in Chapter 4, this had an important part to play in the development of patent law. Judgment was given by the Lord Chief Justice, Sir Alexander Cockburn (1802–80), who concluded:

According to the statute of James, the power of the Crown to grant the right of monopoly in the case of inventions is not to be exercised where public inconvenience would ensue. Now a patentee, having the sole right to the use of his invention, is not bound to permit anyone else to use it; so that, if the Crown were subject to the general restrictions, the state might be deprived of the use of an article essential to the public service— possibly for the defence of the realm—while a foreign power, perhaps an

Amended
Disclaimer, &c.   A.D. 1852.—N° 884*.   7

Feather's Improvements in Ships, rendering them Impervious to Shot.

It would also prevent (if applied to the lower hull inside or between the timbers and the planking outside) any serious consequences of leakage from whatever cause, and altogether render the vessels in every way, and under all circumstances, more safe and comfortable, and insure greater security to those necessarily exposed and
5 jeopardized in time of war.

The same process might be applied for the protection of boats with equal advantage, the proportion and mode of application being somewhat modified to suit the circumstances of the case.

The spikes which secure the caoutchouc or india-rubber lining should be
10 inserted in a sufficiently warm state to admit of their being driven through without actually dissolving the material, which on cooling again would close upon and adhere more firmly to the metal.

The third and last part of my Invention relates to an improved method of constructing the decks of ships or vessels.—The hold and deck beams may be
15 constructed either of timber or iron, and all the decks below the upper or quarter deck are to laid with iron instead of wood as at present.—The decks will then consist of sheets or plates (of adequate thickness) laid with butt or lapped joints, which are to be secured to the horizontal beams, and additionally supported by means of zig-zag or other shaped iron frames, fitted and let in between, and fastened
20 to the several beams, with a strong circular or dove-tailed plate at the respective angles of the frames and spiked down, and so fitted and made flush that the iron deck have an equal and level bearing throughout its whole surface.—This construction will be altogether lighter in structure than the ordinary kind of deck, and would greatly tend to strengthen and stiffen the vessel.—It would also act as a
25 great preservative against the chance of conflagration and the effects of shot, and would not be liable either to rip or splinter, it would also be less costly than the ordinary plan, and would wear an indefinite time, and could be more easily repaired when necessary, and would require no caulking, while at the same time it would save a large expenditure of timber, and be more healthy because more cleanly, and
30 more easily kept so.

Figure 10 is a plan view, and Figure 11 a vertical section of part of a deck shewing some of the iron plates n, n, removed in order that the deck beams and iron zig-zag or other shaped iron framing m, m, may be more clearly seen.

Having now described my various improvements and the best means
35 with which I am at present acquainted for carrying the same into effect, I claim in conclusion, first, the *Invention* method herein described of constructing ships or vessels of wood and iron combined. Second, the method herein described or any mere modification thereof of lining or padding the sides of ships or other vessels and boats, so as to render them more secure and impervious to cannon

FIG. 3. Last two pages of Robert Feather's amended disclaimer (see overleaf)

8   A.D. 1852.—N° 884*.   Amended Disclaimer, &c.

Feather's Improvements in Ships, rendering them Impervious to Shot.

~~shot.—Lastly, I claim constructing the decks of ships or vessels of iron as above shewn and described.~~

In witness whereof, I, the said Robert Barnard Feather, have hereunto set my hand and seal, the Twenty-third day of September, One thousand eight hundred and sixty-three.   5

R. B. FEATHER. (L.S.)

Witness,
    F. PARTRIDGE,
        4, Molyneux Place,
            Water Street,   10
                Liverpool.

To the Commissioners of Patents for Inventions.

I hereby grant my fiat, giving leave to the above-mentioned Robert Barnard Feather to file in the Great Seal Patent Office, with the Specification to which the same relates, the above-written Amended Disclaimer and 15 Memorandum of Alteration.

Lincoln's Inn,   ROUNDELL PALMER.
2nd November 1863.

LONDON:
Printed by GEORGE EDWARD EYRE and WILLIAM SPOTTISWOODE,
Printers to the Queen's most Excellent Majesty. 1863.

enemy, would have full opportunity to profit by the invention (*HPC* 8 at 760).

Feather was most unhappy at losing his case. He wrote a letter to *The Times* (8 Feb. 1865, p. 11), assuring the editor that in future he would keep all his brilliant ideas secret 'rather than submit to such lawless seizure and open defiance of redress'. Although the Admiralty had been advised by a number of experts that Feather's ideas were either obvious or impracticable, they decided to pay him an honorarium of £1,000 and contribute £600 towards his costs. The reason they did this comes out clearly in the report that the solicitor to the Admiralty wrote on the case (PRO: TS45/120):

Feather's continual complaining was spoiling the good relationship that both the War Office and the Admiralty hoped to maintain with inventors.

Let us return to the 1869 debate in the House of Commons on the abolition of the patent system. Sir Roundell Palmer's secondment of the motion was followed by a long speech from Lord Stanley, chairman of the 1864 commission (Section 3.3). Still a Tory at this time, Lord Stanley spoke from the opposition benches, but he was clearly in favour of abolition. He put forward the wisdom of a gradual approach, and reminded the House that there were many voices outside Parliament that would speak up in support of the present system. There were certainly few voices inside Parliament that day to speak up in favour of patents, and the general atmosphere implied that this was just the beginning of the end as far as the United Kingdom's patent system was concerned. Macfie withdrew his motion in the obvious expectation that the government would do something quite soon. This turned out to be the case, as we shall see below, but first let us hear one of the voices outside Parliament to which Lord Stanley referred.

3.5   The Copyright Analogy

One of the most often quoted voices in support of the patent system during the 1860–80 patent controversy was that of John Stuart Mill (1806–73). He had even added to a paragraph of his *Principles of Political Economy*, when the fifth edition came out in 1862, to make his position on patents clear. What Mill wrote is interesting for us today, when copyright and patent right are bundled together as 'intellectual property' and treated in a single Act of Parliament. In the nineteenth century copyright and patent right were covered by different legislation. Copyright in the United Kingdom began seriously with the Act of 1842. What Mill added to his book in 1862 ran as follows:

It is generally admitted that the present Patent Laws need much improvement; but in this case, as well as in the closely analogous one of Copyright, it would be a gross immorality in the law to set everybody free to use a person's work without his consent, and without giving him an equivalent. I have seen with real alarm several recent attempts, in quarters carrying some authority, to impugn the principle of patents altogether; attempts which, if practically successful, would enthrone free stealing under the prostituted name of free trade, and make the men of brains, still more than at present, the needy retainers and dependents of the men of money-bags (Mill (1926), 933).

Mill's hope that a close analogy would develop between the laws governing patent right and copyright has, in many ways, been fulfilled. Today both are found under the general heading of intellectual property rights, and Cornish, at the beginning of his definitive text *Intellectual Property*, states that 'patents, breach of confidence and copyright' are all 'concerned with the protection of ideas' (Cornish (1989), 3). Cornish is equally clear, however, that very different kinds of ideas may be involved. With regard to patents, in modern law a clear procedure is involved in deciding the validity of an idea for the grant of a patent: novelty, inventive step, clear and complete disclosure, and so on (ibid., ch. 5). In the case of modern copyright law there is no such procedure for deciding validity. Only a 'work' and an 'author' who 'creates' are called for. The work does not need to contain new ideas; in fact it need not contain any ideas at all. The 'idea', in the case of copyright, could be how the 'work' is typeset, what it sounds like, how it was photographed, and so on, and the copyright then belongs to the 'creator', which would often be a multinational company (ibid. 266–7, 277).

Mill's own famous work *Principles of Political Economy* serves as an excellent example of just how little ideas of a technical or scientific kind have to do with copyright. Mill continually brings in the ideas of Adam Smith, Thomas De Quincey, and David Ricardo, for example, in his discussion of value (Mill (1926), 436–7), but it seems unlikely that he would have thought he was stealing anything, and of course he was not. It is an author's *text* that is copyright, not the ideas put forward in the text. The text of a patent is also copyright—Crown copyright in the case of the United Kingdom—but patent rights concern the ideas in the text of the patent, no matter how these may be rewritten or expressed in some other way. Mill also used other people's texts in his writing of *Principles of Political Economy*. He reproduced literally page after page from two contemporary books, John Rae's *New Principles of Political Economy* (Boston, 1834) and Charles Babbage's *Economy of Machines and Manufactures* (London, 1834). Both books were published only fourteen years before Mill's first edition. There is, of course, nothing wrong in this. Mill gave the full reference for what he copied, the quotation marks, running on page after page, making it clear that we are not reading Mill, but Rae or Babbage. As Blanco-White and Jacob (1986, p. 151) tell us, the law in Mill's time, as in ours, allows an author to quote an entire book by another author, not only a few pages or a paragraph, provided the quotation is needed to make some point in a scientific text or a critical review, and provided the full reference for the source and the name of the copied author are given: 'What [the copyright holder] cannot do is to prevent readers . . . making use of what they have learnt by reading' (ibid. 164). But this is precisely what the patent right holder *can* do, both in Mill's time and today.

3.6   The Abolitionists Defeated

Macfie may have withdrawn his motion of May 1869, but the select committee he hoped for was appointed within a few days. Macfie was, of course, a member, and he tried unsuccessfully to be elected chairman. In fact, the two massive accounts of the evidence given before the select committee (BPP 1871 (368), x. 603; 1872 (193), xi. 395) show how the abolitionists and their leader, Macfie, were continually outvoted, while those who supported the patent system gathered some outstanding witnesses to support their case. The reason for this was political. The period 1868–74 was the time of the first Gladstone administration, the union of the old Whig party with the free traders and the followers of Sir Robert Peel (1788–1850). This union, representing a union of one part of the old aristocratic ruling class with the new class of powerful manufacturers, had learnt by experience that free trade was a rather idealistic kind of politics. A far better strategy was to use the law to gain a monopoly, and the patent laws were just one aspect of the kind of legal structure that the new Liberals thought was needed. To an old free trader like Macfie this must have seemed incomprehensible.

Three examples of the new philosophy of manufacturing management can be taken from the 1871 and 1872 reports of the select committee. The first is Henry Bessemer (1813–98), the English engineer who held patents on his process for making steel. Bessemer was exceptional among inventors in that he was quite open about the income he received from the royalties on his patents. He told *The Times*, in connection with his knighthood and fellowship of the Royal Society, in 1879, that he had received a total of £1,057,748 from his patents up to then (Macfie (1883), p. lx). Before the select committee, Bessemer spoke with great enthusiasm for the existing patent system. He explained how his steel-making process had been first made public in 1856, and how he had spent the subsequent years perfecting his process and buying up any competing patent rights where these had not, by good luck, lapsed because the inventors concerned had failed to pay their fees. He had ended up with a steelworks of his own in Sheffield, which at the time produced better steel than any other, and the process he used was protected by an unassailable portfolio of patents. His steel was not only the best, it was £20 per ton cheaper. The other steel manufacturers were forced to adopt his process and pay him royalties, even though the Bessemer process was soon to be superseded (*EB*11, 3 at 823).

The second witness who spoke up in favour of the status quo was James Nasmyth (1808–90), the Scottish engineer who was able to retire at the age of 48, with a great fortune, from his foundry at Bridgewater. He is best remembered for his invention of the steam hammer, but his claim for this is as dubious as the claims of most so-called great inventors, particularly in view of the fact that Nasmyth did not actually build a steam hammer until he saw one at work in France in 1842. This is an interesting story and has been told by Cantrell, who has drawn on the archives of both Nasmyth and the great French manufacturers Creuzot-Loire (Cantrell (1984), 134–50). Nasmyth, like Bessemer, was a brilliant engineer but, again like Bessemer, he owed his great wealth far more to his skill in manipulating the patent system than to his skill in mechanical design.

Our third example is Karl Wilhelm Siemens (1823–83), one of the founders of Siemens AG, which today dominates the European electrical industry. He became a British subject in 1859 and, as he explained to the select committee, the reason he settled in England was because of the excellent patent laws which had been introduced by the Act of 1852. He contrasted the situation in England with that in his native Germany, where his brother Werner found the patent situation far more difficult to exploit. Werner was later to play a major part in patent law reform in Germany (Siemens (1966), 234–6).

It is hardly surprising that Bessemer, Nasmyth, and Siemens all spoke up in favour of the existing system of patent law in the United Kingdom. Their respective industries had worked out the best ways of using these laws, and the best ways of employing the patent agents and lawyers to get the results they needed. The case for abolition collapsed, as far as the select committee was concerned, and their final report of 1872 came down strongly in favour of a patent system. If any reform were needed, they argued, it was necessary only to go back to the ideas put forward in 1851 and 1852: proper examination of the specifications, and at last perhaps the government might find the funds for a new building to house the Patent Office and its library.

As Machlup and Penrose (1950) have concluded, the abolitionists had all the good arguments, but they lost the battle for political reasons. Industry at the time needed the protection that a patent system could give: protection against foreign competition and protection from the imitation of products by competitors at home. Used in the correct way, patents could provide the ideal free trade environment: competitors could trade freely once they had paid up the royalties demanded. How much, and what for, was for the holders of the patent rights to decide.

In all the pages of evidence, and in the excellent summary index, of the 1871–2 report from the select committee, there is no mention of our main topic: state secrets. The idea of keeping commercial secrets, as opposed to going to all the trouble of obtaining a patent, was brought up, but only to repeat what had been said in all the previous reports of earlier years. Commercial secrecy was no solution to the problem of gaining a real advantage over one's competitor when one had a new idea.

State secrecy was still on the agenda, however, as the next chapter will show.

4

Towards an Official Secrets Act

4.1   Public Records

The last chapter has taken us as far as 1870 in the history of secret patents, when Parliament was clearly preparing for a change in the patent system. This occurred in 1883, and will be dealt with in this chapter, which will then consider a closely related Act, the Official Secrets Act of 1889. The Public Record Office holds papers concerning the preparation of both Acts, and some of the papers concern discussions and decisions that took place back in the 1870s. This is in great contrast to the situation surrounding the Acts of 1852 and 1859, which were discussed in Chapters 2 and 3: no records survive that might tell us about the confidential discussions that preceded the preparation of these bills.

The Public Record Office was established by Act of Parliament in 1838, so it is not surprising that records of administrative detail are sparse for the earlier years of the nineteenth century. It should also be noted that records were kept secret for fifty years until fairly recently, when the time-delay was reduced to thirty years. Many files may be retained by a department, however, and an interesting example of this concerns the Admiralty papers dealing with a visit of the Soviet warship *Sverdlov* to Spithead in 1953 (PRO: ADM1/27600). Sensitive files may also be released to the PRO and yet remain closed for extended periods. An example is ADM1/27528, which contains papers concerning 'conscientious objectors in the Services: future arrangements' and cannot be seen until the year 2042, when the papers will all be more than seventy-five years old.

Thus records concerning an Act of the 1880s could not be seen by the public before the 1930s. These papers, many of which were confidential at the time, give us a much broader picture of the history of secret patents. Let us begin with a bundle of papers (PRO: WO32/6205) made available to the public in 1928, which deals with the possibility of patent law reform in the years before 1877.

4.2   *C. M. Clode Draws up a Paper*

On 7 December 1876 a seven-page memorandum entitled 'Patents for Inventions: Position of the War Department in regard to Patents for Munitions of War etc.' was printed and sent to a number of departments in Whitehall. It was signed by Brigadier-General F. A. Campbell, director of artillery at the War Office, whose preamble referred to the reports from the Royal Commission of 1864, and the findings of the 1871–2 select committee. No changes in the patent law had yet been made, he pointed out, and problems still remained (PRO: WO32/6205). The Brigadier-General then referred to a letter of 14 January 1875 from the Lord Chancellor to the Secretary of State for War, asking for his opinion of the usefulness of the 1859 Act. Should this kind of legislation be repeated in the new patent law that was now being framed? The answer from the War Office had been 'that no benefit had resulted from the Act in question', but it becomes clear, on reading through the memorandum, that the 'benefit' hoped for was not greater secrecy but some help in avoiding the payment of royalties.

C. M. Clode, the solicitor to the War Office, had drawn up a paper for the Lord Chancellor in answer to his question which was attached to the Brigadier-General's memorandum. In his paper Clode made specific reference to Sir William Armstrong's patent for rifled ordnance, BPN 611 of 1859, one of the very first patents to be 'kept secret' under the 1859 Act, as we saw in Chapter 3. Clode wrote:

In Sir William Armstrong's case the Department was relieved from all embarrassment by his placing his Patent at the disposal of the Crown, but the official minutes written when this concession was made (see the late Mr. Godley's minute annexed) show that the Crown was entirely at his mercy, and that any sum he had asked for, the Crown would have been obliged to give in the then unsettled state of public affairs (PRO: WO32/ 6205).

The 'then unsettled state' was, of course, the Crimean War. But when the War Department is euphemistically termed the 'Defence Department', it is not easy for today's reader to see what the problem was in 1859. Why not threaten Armstrong with the Tower of London, along the lines of Klaus Fuchs? The late Godley's minute referred to by Clode gives us the answer: Armstrong was a gentleman, not a mere employee. What Godley had written, on 15 December 1858 was:

It must not be forgotten that Mr Armstrong has acted with a liberality and confidence in us which entitles him to a full reciprocation. If he chose to ask the Government for £100,000 within a week, with the alternative of offering his invention to a foreign Government, no one can doubt but that the money would be paid *at once*. Mr Armstrong waives any condition of personal remuneration, and taking this into consideration, we cannot be wrong in placing ourselves to some extent in his hands (PRO: WO32/6205).

4.3 Real Estate

These opinions from two War Office solicitors (for Godley was Clode's predecessor) show that Armstrong's intellectual property rights were being taken seriously. The point was that the 1859 Act only laid down a *procedure* whereby a patent could be assigned to the Crown and then kept secret. If the patentee did not agree to enter this procedure, there was little that the Crown could do. Clode made this clear in his paper. He contrasted intellectual property and real estate, because there *was* an Act of Parliament that allowed the Crown to take over a gentleman's real estate when this was needed for defence purposes. Why not, he argued, have a similar arrangement for intellectual property?

The Act that Clode referred to was the Defence Act of 1842 (5 & 6 Vict., c. 94), the full title of which was 'An Act to consider and amend the Laws relating to the Services of the Ordnance Department, and the vesting and purchase of Lands and Hereditaments for those Services, and for the Defence and Security of the Realm'. The kind of problem this Act was intended to solve was the provision of land for artillery ranges, for troop exercises, for billeting troops, or for manœuvres. Section 19 of the Act, Clode explained, illustrated 'that for the defence of the realm the powers of the Crown should remain entirely unfettered'. It laid down the procedure for taking over real estate without notice, and putting it to the use that the defence of the realm required, 'and afterwards, not before', as Clode put it, 'a jury can be summoned to assess the price or compensation to be paid to the land owner'. This was the way, he argued, to deal with intellectual property rights when they were needed for defence purposes. Take over the patent rights and then, 'afterwards, not before', get some independent assessor to decide what, if any, compensation might be due.

We shall see, later in this chapter, that Clode's idea was taken up in the new patent law of 1883. It is important to note, however, that his idea is of no help at all to a government that wishes to keep secrets. It is not possible to take over a person's property secretly, without their agreement, unless legislation allows that the person is taken over as well. An independent assessor is not going to help with the problem. Secrecy was not the problem Clode was dealing with here; he was concerned with intellectual property rights. Let us now look at whether any attempt was made to keep technical ideas secret in the armed forces and armament factories of Great Britain during the latter part of the nineteenth century.

4.4   Secrecy

Secrecy is not discussed in any of the papers under PRO: WO32/6205. All the letters, minutes, and reports consider the questions of reducing costs and avoiding the payment of royalties. The case of *Feather* v. *Regina* (see Chapter 3) had established, for the time being, that a patentee could not use his patent rights 'against the Crown', but this was a difficult principle to impose when the Crown made use of armaments, or simply supplies, that were manufactured by private industry and also supplied to private customers or to foreign governments.

The question of secrecy does come up in the papers found in another bundle, PRO: WO32/6206, which deals with the framing of the Patents, Designs and Trade Marks Act of 1883 (46 & 47 Vict., c. 57) and its later effects. This bundle was made available to the public in 1936. It contains a long manuscript by Sir Frederick Abel (1827–1902), who was chief chemist to the War Office from 1854 to 1888 and is remembered for his outstanding work on explosives, which he undertook with James Dewar (1842–1923), Cambridge professor of low-temperature fame.

Sir Frederick's manuscript, dated 20 August 1888, complains bitterly that research and development work on explosives in France and Germany is done 'in almost complete secrecy'. In the United Kingdom, in contrast, everything seemed to get into the newspapers because 'practical work must be carried out upon some open space in the [Woolwich] Arsenal, to all parts of which Newspaper Reporters and their Agents have free access'. Sir Frederick continued with a clear suggestion that outsiders could easily have a good look around the arsenal, and then go home and take out a patent on whatever they had seen being developed. While this seems rather over-anxious on his part, it suggests that things were surprisingly open at the Woolwich Arsenal in his time, and this may be confirmed from another source. In the first edition of the *Blue Guide to London* (London, 1920), there is an extraordinary passage to be found within the pages describing Woolwich and Greenwich, the most easterly parts of London that lie on the south bank of the Thames. The subject is the possibility of a visit to the Royal Arsenal:

Before the War [1914–18] visitors were admitted [to the Woolwich Arsenal] by tickets obtained from the War Office or from the Chief Superintendent (foreigners through their ambassadors) and were conducted around the chief departments: the Gun Factory, founded in 1716; the Carriage Factory, where military vehicles of all kinds are made; the Laboratory for the manufacture of shells and small-arm ammunition; the Army Ordnance Department; and the Naval Ordnance Department (p. 435).

If that was the situation prior to 1914, we may assume that things were just as relaxed in 1888, when Sir Frederick wrote his manuscript.

The open access to the Royal Ordnance factories may be looked upon in another way, however. To allow an outside observer, who may possibly be an agent for a potential enemy, simply to see the manufacture of, for example, 300 millimetre guns for the British Navy, and to note that these guns are rifled, right-hand screw-sense, and are about 10 metres long, is not to give away any great secret. It could be very good propaganda. What would be secret is the kind of alloy steel the British are using, and how well the guns perform under simulated battle conditions. Just looking around the factory, provided the visitor is not allowed to pick up any swarf or scrap, is not going to give any answers to those kinds of questions.

It so happens that we have a very sharp-minded observer of military matters to tell us about the new developments in ordnance in the mid-nineteenth century: Frederick Engels. Engels wrote a series of articles for the *New York Daily Tribune* in April and May 1860 entitled 'Rifled Ordnance', in which he gave the historical background to the important innovations that Armstrong and Whitworth had just made. The new Armstrong gun, Engels wrote, had performed to the great satisfaction of the War Office, and this had been reported to Parliament (H3, 156 at 1295). Engels went on to comment that 'the scientifically interesting details of all these experiments were studiously kept secret'.

4.5   The Act of 1883

C. M. Clode's paper was drawn up in 1875, but nothing happened in the way of patent law reform for many years. In the years of Disraeli's second Tory administration, 1874–80, there were several new bills introduced into Parliament for patent law reform, and many interesting debates, but nothing was changed. There was an interesting debate in the Lords in 1875, when a new bill was introduced by the Lord Chancellor, the distinguished judge Lord Cairns (1819–85). The new bill proposed a proper examination of the specifications that applicants for patents submitted, and this work was to be done by 'men of scientific and manufacturing eminence', the Lord Chancellor explained, who would be 'willing, as a mark of distinction [that is, without payment], to serve on the Commission and perform the duties that will be imposed upon them' (H3, 222 at 250).

This desperation to avoid any expense in operating the patent system runs through all the debates of the 1870s. The Lord Chancellor concluded his introduction of the new bill by listing the large staff established in the US Patent Office in Washington, DC at the time. Nothing of the kind was going to happen in the United Kingdom, he assured their lordships. Further ridicule of the US patent system came in the debate on the 1875 bill, after its second reading in the Lords. Viscount Cardwell cited US patents on spittoons, and one for sticking a slip of sandpaper inside one's hat for the purpose of striking matches (H3, 222 at 916–41). In the event, nothing came of the 1875 bill, and the same was true of bills introduced in 1876 and 1877. Things did not start moving in the area of patent law reform until the Liberals took over again, from 1880 to 1885. This was Gladstone's second administration, and his President of the Board of Trade was Joseph Chamberlain (1836–1914).

There was a debate on patent law reform in the Commons on 15 June 1881, and Chamberlain's contribution to it (H3, 258 at 586–90) was, first, to remind the House of the abolition movement, which had been so strong some fifteen years earlier. This, he said, was now completely dead. He went on to make it clear that, if the previous Tory administration had been in favour of leaving the patent law as it was, the new Liberal government favoured only the minimum of reform. All the agitation for a proper examination of patent applications, for example, Chamberlain thought quite foolish: just look at the United States, where examinations were made. Nearly all the patents there, he declared, had been copied from British ideas, and yet the US examiners passed all the old British ideas as new ones! Chamberlain was to exhibit a similar arrogance again during the debate on the 1883 bill (H3, 278 at 358).

By 1883 there were no fewer than three bills for patent law reform before Parliament, one of these being from the government. The private members' bills were soon withdrawn, and the government bill extended to combine all the old legislation covering patents, designs, and trade marks. This progressed very smoothly through the Commons, and when it came before the Lords for its second reading the debate was led by the Lord Chancellor, the Earl of Selborne. He was, of course, Roundell Palmer, who, as we saw earlier, was changed by his experience from being a strong supporter of patent rights in 1851 to being strongly in favour of complete abolition of the patent system in 1869. In 1883 the Lord Chancellor did just mention his recollection of a movement for abolition, many years ago, but went on to say that 'public opinion had not yet proved favourable to any change in that direction' (H3, 282 at 2034). The bill was given royal assent on 25 August 1883.

The Patents, Designs and Trade Marks Act of 1883 (46 & 47 Vict., c. 57) abolished the old commissioners of patents and set up a comptroller-general for the Patent Office. There was a clear intention to provide the comptroller with a new building and more staff. These were needed to carry through the major tasks of publishing all the old specifications, with abridgements, and setting up a sophisticated classification and indexing system that would then be used to carry on the work with the ever-increasing number of applications. We shall see, in Chapter 6, that all these plans were fulfilled.

Two major changes in the patent law were made by the 1883 Act. The first concerned the objections that could be made against a patent application. Section 11 of the 1883 Act now set a period of two months between the acceptance of a complete specification and the sealing of the patent, and during this period the complete specification was open to inspection by the public. Anyone could object during the time but, unlike the Act of 1852, the grounds for objection were clearly defined. One could object on the most obvious ground, that the invention had been stolen from one, but also 'on the ground that the invention had been patented in this country in an application of prior date, or on the ground of an examiner having reported to the comptroller that the specification appears to him to comprise the same invention as is comprised in a specification bearing the same or similar title and accompanying a previous application, *but on no other ground*' (emphasis added). Thus the entirely open grounds of 1852 were abolished and, even worse for a government that might wish to keep secrets, the statute laid down that the specification had to be open to public inspection for two months.

The second major change made by the Act of 1883 was set out in section 27. This is worth quoting in full because it followed the proposal Clode had made in his 1875 paper, using the analogy of real estate (see Section 4.3). It was introduced, however, with another new idea which made a change in the opposite direction. It is surprising that the Lord Chancellor had made no mention of this point, because it reversed the decision of the famous case of *Feather* v. *Regina*, in which he had played a major role. Section 27 of the 1883 Act ran as follows:

(1) A patent shall have to all intents the like effect as against Her Majesty the Queen, her heirs and successors, as it has against a subject.

(2) But the officers or authorities administering any department of the service of the Crown may, by themselves, their agents, contractors, or others, at any time after the application, use the invention for the services of the Crown on terms to be before or after the use thereof agreed on, with the approval of the Treasury, between these officers or authorities and the patentee, or, in default of such agreement, on such terms as may be settled by the Treasury after hearing all parties concerned.

The first paragraph is very important because it meant that a royalty could now be extracted from a Royal Ordnance factory when it was being used to manufacture anything covered by a valid patent. In the case of *Feather* v. *Regina*, Feather had lost because the principle was put forward that the Crown had a prerogative to defend the realm that could not be interfered with. The first paragraph of section 27 reversed this decision. It made it clear that, as far as a subject's patent rights were concerned, the Crown must show the same respect as anyone.

The second paragraph qualified this new idea, however, and in just the way Clode had suggested in his 1875 paper. His 'after, not before' principle is here, but his idea of an independent arbitrator, who would decide what compensation might be due to the patentee, has been replaced with the somewhat less independent Treasury. In this way the government could be certain of getting a reasonable bargain.

4.6 Secrecy in the Act of 1883

There was no mention of secrecy or security problems in the 1883 debates. The Act of 1883 simply took the procedure laid down by the Patents for Inventions (Munitions of War) Act of 1859, and put this into section 44 of the new Act. When a patent was assigned to the Secretary of State for War for the purpose of keeping it secret, section 44 laid down that 'the application and specification . . . and drawings, shall, instead of being left in the ordinary manner at the patent office, be delivered to the comptroller in a packet sealed by authority of the Secretary of State'.

A conference was held at the War Office on 15 June 1891 to consider how the 1883 Act was working out from their point of view, and the confidential report of the proceedings survives (PRO: WO32/6206). It tells us how many patents the various government departments had taken out since 1883, and how many of these were kept secret by means of section 44 of the Act. The War Office had taken out a total of sixty-seven patents since the new law had come into force eight years previously, and only three of these had been kept secret. The report tells us the names of the patentees involved, and the dates and subjects of the patent applications. What is perhaps surprising is that these names and subjects can today be found in the printed index to British patents, for the same dates concerned, which suggests that the patents were not kept secret after all, and can be found in the bound copies of patent specifications available in many public libraries.

However, readers will be disappointed. Should they care to look up Patent No. 6168 of 1886, to M. T. Sale, entitled 'Improvements in Land Torpedoes', or No. 5614 of 1889, to F. A. Abel and J. Dewar, entitled 'An Improvement in the Manufacture of Explosives for Ammunition', they will find a slip of paper bound in place of the specification headed 'Memorandum to Librarians'. It states that 'The Publication of this Specification is in abeyance under Section 44, Sub-section 10, of the Patents, Designs, and Trade Marks Act, 1883.'

The conference also discussed the problem of patents being taken out by officers who were in the manufacturing and experimental departments of the army. Documents in the file (PRO: WO32/6206) tell us that, in 1872, a regulation, that is an entry in the legal code of the army, had been made 'forbidding patents' to members of the army, but there were legal problems in using this. It was also of no help at all in preventing Crown employees from taking out patents. The conference appears to have spent most of its time in a discussion about the design of a form that could be used by employees of the Admiralty, War Office, and Post Office to seek permission to make an application for a patent. A different form would, of course, be needed for each department. While it was thought difficult to withhold from employees the right to apply for patents, failure to apply for permission on the correct form could be made an offence against the conditions of employment.

4.7 *The Official Secrets Act of 1889*

There have been a number of books written about the history of the Official Secrets Acts of the British government. The Act of 1889 was only the first one. Rosamund Thomas (1991) gives a very thorough review of the Acts of 1911, 1920, 1939, and 1989 (the most recent), pointing out that 1889 was a rather ill-framed and cumbersome first attempt. She attributes the origin of the 1889 Act to 'late nineteenth century . . . outbreaks of both unauthorised disclosures and espionage' which occurred in the United Kingdom. A strong case for this has also been made by Aitken (1971), Hooper (1987), and Williams (1965).

The Official Secrets Act of 1889 (52 & 53 Vict., c. 52) dealt with two kinds of offence: being found in a prohibited place, and passing secret information to a third party. It did not have a peaceful passage through Parliament, because it appeared to many MPs, and to many noble lords, to make ill-defined actions criminal offences. For example, as Dr Charles Cameron, MP for Glasgow College, put it: 'The Bill provides that if any man in government office disclose an official secret contrary to the rules of the office —which by the way may be modified and altered at any time without the cognizance of this House—he shall be liable to certain penalties.' This, he rightly pointed out, could be used to prevent MPs being given information that they might need to fulfil their representative obligations. Cameron had more to say, however, and he went on to argue, in a rather roundabout way, that an Official Secrets Act like this one could be used to cover up the fact that 'inventions may be pirated, and in fact we know how in the Post Office certain telegraphic inventions are pirated'. For this remark he was called to order by the Speaker (H3, 335 at 1074). What he was referring to was the fact that the British Post Office manufactured much of its own equipment at the time. If a description of the equipment in use were made an official secret, how could the holder of a patent that might then be infringed get to know about it?

The connection between the Official Secrets Act and patents came up in another remark during the passage of the bill, this time from the Attorney-General himself, just before the Commons passed the bill on to the Lords. On 20 June 1889 the Attorney-General was asked about the possibility that evidence of bad management in a government department could be made an official secret, and thus be covered up. He replied that this was impossible to avoid, and gave an example to show that official secrets were more important than good management: 'When it was decided to adopt a new system of guns the fact was made known, very much to the detriment of the War Department, who had to pay a larger price for the new patent than they would otherwise have had to pay' (H3, 337 at 320). Here was a clear example of the connection between official secrets and reducing public expenditure, clearer even than Cameron's, but the Speaker did not call the Attorney-General to order. The bill received royal assent on 26 August 1889.

A major work on secrecy in the United Kingdom (Andrew (1985)) points out the difficulties that researchers have with the public records in this area. Any references to the Official Secrets

Acts, of various vintages, seem to have been weeded out. There is one bundle of papers (PRO: WO32/6347) that is concerned with the framing of the 1889 Act, and this was opened to the public in 1946. The papers discuss legal problems and the kind of penalties, for example penal servitude for life, that should be imposed upon soldiers caught selling information to spies. Another bundle (PRO: WO32/6173) deals with 'custody and disposal of secret documents' for the 1890s. This was made public in 1942 and is concerned with entirely routine matters.

Among the papers in the Public Record Office that deal with patents, however, we do find the 1889 Act mentioned. In one large bundle, PRO: WO32/6206, there is a long memorandum, dated 17 July 1890, from the director of artillery at the War Office, Brigadier-General H. J. Alderson. It concerns the embarrassment the War Office suffered because of BPN 1115 of 1889, entitled 'Improvements in or relating to the Manufacture and Treatment of Explosives'. This patent had been first applied for in January 1889 by one H. M. Chapman, an analytical chemist from Waltham Cross, and accepted. The complete specification was published in May 1890. The Brigadier-General was careful not to go into technical details in his memorandum, but, reading between the lines, it seems certain that Chapman's patent described the same process that was described in the secret patent of Abel and Dewar, BPN 5614 of 1889 (see Section 4.6).

As Chapman was a private citizen, and his patent application had been made earlier than Abel and Dewar's, the whole matter was indeed embarrassing to the War Office. The Brigadier-General commented:

I cannot but think that the only way to prevent a recurrence of such an incident . . . would be to have some means of examining specifications applied for, as has been from time to time advocated by this Department. At present we have no machinery for such a purpose . . . and we may only be made aware by accident of applications to which objection should be made. This I consider very important, particularly when it is remembered that, as has been stated by the Law Officers, such examination is the only means by which the taking out of open patents for inventions the specifications of which have been sealed up on representation of the Secretary of State can be prevented.

What Alderson is saying here is that not only have there been cases like Chapman's, where a patent has been applied for by a private citizen just before the same idea was put forward by government workers, but there have also been cases where an outsider has got hold of, or perhaps independently invented, some idea that was already described in one of the government's secret patents. Alderson's mention of the law officers is also significant because it connects with some remarks in a letter, dated 17 March 1894, from the War Office to the Admiralty (PRO: ADM116/327). This tells us that the law officers were consulted about the right of the Crown to inspect provisional specifications in the Patent Office during the period when the applicant was under the impression that his work was being kept confidential. The law officers' answer was that the Crown had no such right, because the 1883 Act, by means of the first part of section 27 (see Section 4.5), 'was intended to put the Crown in the same general position as the public'.

Put together, Alderson's memorandum of 1890 and the War Office letter of 1894 might cause a reader with a suspicious turn of mind to imagine that *before* 1883 it had been taken for granted that the royal prerogative to defend the realm (established, as far as patent rights were concerned, by *Feather* v. *Regina* in 1865) *had* given the Crown the right to read provisional, and complete, specifications as soon as these were filed, if it was thought necessary. After 1883, when section 11 of the Act had laid all specifications open to inspection for two months before sealing, and section 27 had put the Crown on the same footing as anyone else, it was surely impossible for the Crown to get at any secrets, and then keep them.

Alderson's remark about 'open patents' could be taken to suggest that he understood that the Official Secrets Act of 1889 had now given the War Office the right to see specifications, when these were still meant to be confidential, in cases where there was reason to suspect that an offence, under the Act, may have occurred. We shall see in Chapter 6 that there is no evidence that irregularities of this kind ever occurred, but there was clearly a contradiction between the Acts of 1883 and 1889. The Act of 1883 put a statutory obligation on the comptroller-general to publish a specification, while the Act of 1889 could make the very act of publication an offence. Alderson's closing remarks on this topic reveal that he had problems with the Official Secrets Act anyway: prosecution was going to make public what the secret was. As he put it: 'The difficulty . . . as to obtaining a conviction under the Official Secrets Act in consequence of it being left to a Jury to decide whether the information ought or ought not to be communicated "at that time" opens up a very important question, as to whether the Act is really operative or not.'

4.8   Conclusions

This chapter has taken us almost to the end of the nineteenth century. The new building for the Patent Office and its library, completed in 1895, stands ready for the busy century to come. Before we continue, it may be a good idea to take a short break and look at what happened when some inventors offered the British government secrets that were of some potential: the secrets of two major technical revolutions (Constant (1980)) that took place, one just before the turn of the century, and the other just after.

5

The Secrets of Two Technical
Revolutions

5.1   The Beginnings of Wireless Telegraphy

In February 1896 Guglielmo Marconi (1874–1937) sailed from Italy
to England with his mother. He brought with him his experimental
equipment for wireless telegraphy, and the plan was to contact
some wealthy people with whom his mother was connected and
persuade them to provide capital for the exploitation of his ideas
(Marconi (1962), 33; Baker (1970), 28; Jolly (1972), 34). The
Marconis first lived in one of the apartments that Sophia Gerstner
rented out at 71 Hereford Road, in a part of London then called
Westbourne Park, a large-scale speculative development of ter-
raced family houses that had been built around 1850. 'Until 1830
this was one of the most beautiful rural spots for which the parish
of Paddington was renowned' (Clunn (1932), 385). Perhaps the
speculative builders hoped that its glorious past would ensure a
glorious future, but by 1896 the houses were nearly all in multiple
occupation. The railway into Paddington station had been widened considerably, so that the street in Westbourne Park in which
Thomas Hardy (1840–1928) had lived from 1863 to 1874 had been
demolished on one side. If Hardy had still lived there, he would
have looked out of his house across a narrow road to see nothing
but a plain brick wall.

Why did the well-connected Mrs Marconi choose to live in such
poor surroundings? Why do we find Marconi giving a whole list of
addresses in this area over the next eighteen months: 21 Burlington
Road, now completely demolished; 67 Talbot Road, just round
the corner from a final address, again in Hereford Road at 101?
The explanation is almost certainly the kind of work Marconi
needed the rooms for. Perhaps his mother was left at No. 71 while
Guglielmo took the other rooms for his work, perhaps following
complaints from Mrs Gerstner as to the noise and smell of his

spark-gaps. She was probably also unhappy about the continuous deliveries of electric batteries that Marconi would have arranged, for there was no electricity supplied to the houses. The problem of electric power for Marconi's experiments may also explain the choice of Westbourne Park in the first place. A new electric power station had been built in the area in 1886 by the Great Western Railway to supply the electric lighting of the main terminus, with its hotel and offices, and also the lighting at two small stations on the main line, Royal Oak and Westbourne Park (Parsons (1939), ch. 3). The house in Burlington Road that Marconi used was very close to the railway and he may have hoped for, or perhaps obtained, some kind of electricity supply for his work.

Having set the London scene upon which this energetic young man operated, let us look at some of the documents that tell us what he did.

5.2   Marconi's Letter to the War Office

Marconi's good relationship with William Preece, the chief engineer of the British Post Office, and the story of the development of wireless telegraphy, have been clearly presented by Marconi's biographers (Marconi (1962); Baker (1970); Jolly (1972)). Demonstrations of Marconi's equipment were made over land and at sea during 1896, and a public lecture and demonstration in December 1896 brought him a good press. By July 1897, he had founded the company that was to become Marconi's Wireless Telegraph Company in 1900, and which bore that name until 1963.

Marconi left the provisional specification of his first patent (BPN 12039 of 1896) at the Patent Office on 2 June 1896. The patent was mainly concerned with his development of the coherer type of wireless telegraphy receiver (Marconi's version of this involved an important inventive step that will be considered in some detail in Section 5.3). A few days before taking his provisional specification to the Patent Office, he wrote a letter to the War Office which reveals that he had a second line of thought for the development of his ideas: remote control. Telegraphy was clearly his main concern in all his dealings with William Preece and the Post Office, and it also comes over as his main concern in all the public lectures and demonstrations that we find described by his biographers. However, what was happening in the rooms of the various houses in Westbourne Park, and what visitors Marconi saw there, have been somewhat neglected. Let us begin by quoting Marconi's letter in full.

The handwritten letter (PRO: WO32/8594) is dated 20 May 1896, and is addressed to 'The Right Honourable Lord Her Majesty's Principal Secretary of State for War Affairs'. The over-politeness is the first clue we have that Marconi may have decided to write the letter without taking any advice from his mother's well-connected friends. Why he may have done so will be considered below. The letter itself runs as follows:

My Lord,

I Guglielmo Marconi of Bologna (Italy) now residing at 71 Hereford Road, Bayswater [*sic*], W. London do hereby declare that I have discovered electrical devices which enable me to guide or steer a self propelled boat or torpedo from the shore or from a vessel without any person being on board the said boat or torpedo.

It is not necessary to have any communication whatever such as wires or ropes between the self propelled boat or torpedo and the person directing its evolution.

I have found it possible by turning the handle of a simple apparatus of my invention to turn about, steer or enable the independent boat or torpedo to pursue any object at more than a mile from the shore or ship from which it has been launched provided the boat or torpedo has an apparatus of my invention applied to its rudder.

Should your Lordship consider my invention useful to Her Majesty's Army or Navy I am willing to demonstrate its practicability at my own expense, by means of a small self propelled boat on any lake or river where Your Lordship may desire.

I humbly beg Your Lordship to honour me as soon as possible with an answer as I propose otherwise to obtain patents for my discovery and apply it to commercial purposes.

I have the honour to be my Lord your most
      obedient Servant
         G. Marconi.

He was, in fact, writing to the fifth Marquess of Lansdowne (1845–1927). The letter suggests that Marconi may have hoped for some kind of patronage from the British government which would have enabled him to carry on with his experimental work without having to worry about 'commercial purposes'. He had already tried to interest the Italian government along these lines without success (Baker (1970), 28).

The second paragraph of Marconi's letter suggests a connection with a previous case of patronage by the British government. His emphasis that his system will make it unnecessary 'to have any . . . wires or ropes' reminds us that the torpedo that was in use by the British at the time needed precisely that. This was the Brennan torpedo, both guided and powered by wires running back to the shore (Gray (1975), 132–3). Louis Brennan (1852–1936) was a prolific Irish inventor who went to Australia as a child. He offered his torpedo (BPN 3359 of 1877) to the British government in 1881, and made such a good impression on the authorities that the inspector-general of fortifications, writing to the surveyor-general on 17 July 1882, declared that they should 'secure him permanently for the service of the Queen' (PRO: TS21/55). This was done by giving Brennan an honorarium of £5,000 and a permanent job, as superintendent of the 'Brennan Factory' in Gillingham, Kent at a salary of £1,000 per annum (PRO: WO32/8591).

Brennan's torpedo was being abandoned around the time Marconi wrote to the War Office, and it is possible that he knew this and hoped to strike a deal in 1896 along the same lines as Brennan had done in 1882. This possibility is suggested in a four-page report written by one of the War Office experts who visited Marconi's rooms at Westbourne Park on 18 June 1896 (PRO: WO32/8594). Marconi demonstrated his transmitter and receiver, transmitting from one side of the room to the other and from a different room. His wish to apply his ideas in two separate fields—data communications for commercial exploitation, and remote control for military applications—came across clearly to the War Office visitor and was reported. Marconi demonstrated remote control by showing the visitor what today we would describe as a 'pecker motor' being driven one step at a time by one operation of the transmitter's Morse key.

The War Office visitor went on to report that Marconi also claimed that his remote control system would still work when the receiver was inside a closed metal box and under water. This is surprising because it is clearly a false claim: Marconi was using very short wavelengths in these early experiments. Baker (1970, p. 29) also thinks that the idea of underwater communication was 'wholly beyond the capabilities of the Marconi apparatus at that time', referring now to the Salisbury Plain demonstrations that Marconi made later in 1896.

The visitor concluded his report: 'The telegraphic invention would appear to be the most important at present, especially with reference to communications between Lightships and Lighthouses and the shore, and also for military purposes.' No recommendation was made, however, to secure Marconi permanently for the service of the Queen, as had been made for Brennan. It seems possible that Marconi would have much preferred such an arrangement, in contrast to the commercial career that he was pushed into by his financial backers. This possibility is supported by a letter he wrote to Preece in April 1897, which is analysed and discussed by Jolly (1972, pp. 47–9). Marconi had been persuaded to sign an agreement in which he gave away all his past and future patent rights in exchange for half the shares in the new company his financial backers had just set up. He wrote to tell Preece what had happened, and concluded his letter by saying that he would remember the kindness Preece had shown him all his life and would also do all he could 'to keep the company on amicable terms with the British government'. Preece's reply made it clear that he was far from pleased (Jolly (1972), 48).

5.3   Marconi's Patent No. 12039 of 1896

The patent Marconi applied for on 2 June 1896 was the first patent, anywhere, in the field of wireless telegraphy (Baker (1970), 28). For this reason he had to go into considerable technical detail in his specification. He described a new arrangement of components, all of which were familiar to workers in the field of cable telegraphy, and in the field of electricity in general, but his claims were about what the new *system* could do and, in particular, about the way he used a bistable electrical device, the coherer, as a receiver for wireless telegraphy signals. A coherer is an evacuated tube containing two electrodes separated by loosely packed metal powder. The device has two stable electrical states, conducting and non-conducting. It is put into the conducting state by means of a high voltage pulse applied across the two electrodes, and it is put into the non-conducting state by means of a mechanical shock applied to the whole device.

Marconi was not the first to use the coherer as a detector of electromagnetic waves, but he may have been the first to understand (and certainly the first to apply for a British patent on) the

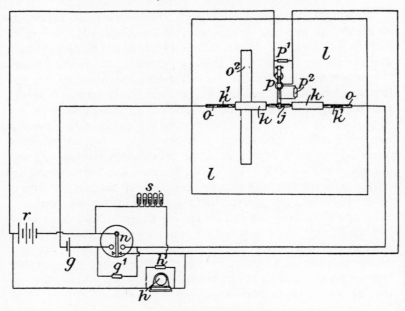

FIG. 4(*a*). Figure from Marconi's specification, BPN 12039 of 1896

way feedback could be used to turn this bistable into a monostable: a device with two states but only one input, which will flip into one state for a short time when an input pulse arrives and then flop back into its normal state. The way Marconi made the bistable coherer into a monostable is shown in Fig. 4. Fig. 4(*a*) is from Marconi's patent and shows his attempt to combine a mechanical drawing (a drawing showing the geometrical relationships between things) with a circuit diagram (a drawing showing the connections between things—the topology). It looks complicated but the important feature is the feedback, which is shown in the simplified diagram in Fig. 4(*b*). Here Marconi's very high frequency dipole aerial (*k–k* in Fig. 4(*a*)) has been replaced by a simple aerial, *A*, and earth connection. When a signal is received, which puts the coherer, *C*, into the conducting state, a small current flows around the circuit formed by the battery, V_1, the coherer, the radio frequency choke, *RFC*, and the relay, *R*. The relay closes and turns on a much larger current, powered by the battery, V_2, which can operate a Morse recorder. In the 1896 diagram this recorder is

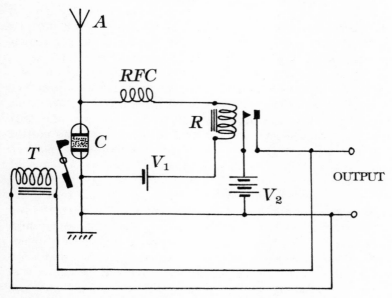

FIG. 4(*b*). Simplification of Marconi's figure showing the feedback path

represented by the object *h*. In the simplified diagram the recorder is not shown, but it would be connected to the output terminals.

Marconi was using the relay, *R*, as a power amplifier for the weak wireless telegraphy signal. He was able to make use of the same kind of sensitive relay that had been used for many years in cable telegraphy for the same task of power amplification. The device was called a relay, and the same name is given to such an electromechanical device today, because it received the weak telegraph signal remaining after a long journey along a cable, and passed it on, restored to full strength, to the next section of cable.

Marconi's inventive step was to feed back some of the amplified signal to his input device, *C*. The feedback path is shown in Fig. 4(*b*) as two leads running back from the output to the electromechanical tapper, *T*. Each time a signal impulse was received by the aerial, the coherer went into the conducting state, the relay closed, and a strong output signal was available. Some of this output was then fed back to the tapper, giving a mechanical shock to the coherer and resetting it to its high impedance state ready for the next impulse to be received. For all this to work properly there had to be the correct time-delay between the coherer going into its conducting state and the tapper putting it back into its non-conducting state. Time-delays were already in Marconi's system: the relay took a finite time to operate, as did the tapper, and we shall see how these times could be adjusted. What comes across very clearly from reading the specification, which was Marconi's first technical publication for it ends with his name and not the name of a patent agent, is that Marconi is a systems engineer. Perhaps one of the first systems engineers, he understood how the whole could be more than the sum of its parts.

To see how Marconi's system worked, we should turn to his own diagram in Fig. 4(a). The coherer is j, set between the two elements of a dipole aerial, k–k. Marconi used such a very high frequency aerial in his first demonstrations, complete with a parabolic reflector, which is shown as l in the figure. The radio frequency chokes are labelled k^1, the relay is n, and the tapper is p. Marconi's circuit also shows damping resistors, g^1, h^1, and p^2, which can be used to adjust the critical time-delays discussed above. Other components, p^1 and s, have been added to give further possibilities for time-delay adjustment and to contain high frequency currents that would be generated by the opening and closing of the relay contacts, and could cause trouble.

All this detail was well explained in Marconi's complete specification, and a blow-up of the region between the dipole elements in the figure was given to show how the whole set-up was supported by the parts labelled o and o^2. It is clear that we are reading about a very complex system that has been worked on at great length and developed into just what Marconi wanted. This is in great contrast to the kind of thought experiments that John Macintosh was writing about (see Chapter 2) and Robert Feather was urgently crossing out (Chapter 3). Marconi was writing about hardware he had put together, and made to work, with his own hands. All the parts that Marconi used, dipole aerials, reflectors, coherers, relays, resistors, capacitors, and electromagnets, were familiar devices in 1896. They had been around, used by telegraph engineers, for decades. What Marconi did was build a new system using these parts, and put the system to a new use. The key inventive step was the feedback loop, involving a time-delay, which reset the coherer to its non-conducting state, so that it was ready for the next impulse to be received. This enabled the Marconi system to work a Morse recorder so that the dots and dashes of the Morse code came out clearly on the paper tape, just as they did with the well-established cable telegraph. This had not been done before with wireless telegraphy.

5.4   Examination by Men of Scientific Eminence

Whenever the proposal that patent applications be examined to see if the ideas put forward were both new and useful was incorporated into a new bill for patent law reform, Parliament greeted it with mixed feelings, and always threw it out of the final Act, either because of the expense or because nobody had a clear picture of how it might be done. This contradiction was not resolved until well into the twentieth century, as we shall see in Chapter 6.

Marconi's patent No. 12039 gives us an example of what can happen when a patent is examined by 'men of scientific and manufacturing eminence', as we saw the Lord Chancellor proposing back in 1875 (see Section 4.5). This occurred because, as Jolly has explained:

In 1900 Whitehall laid plans for a determined attack on Marconi's Company by either having its patents declared invalid or by getting around them with the use of similar, but legally different, apparatus. The Post Office secretly commissioned Professors Oliver Lodge and Silvanus P. Thompson to examine these two possibilities, their reports and all related correspondence being treated as strictly confidential (Jolly (1972), 87–8).

Fortunately 'their reports and all related correspondence' survive today in the Public Record Office (PRO: ADM116/570), and in his book Jolly gives a detailed analysis of the material, quoting at length from the report that Captain Jackson of the Royal Navy wrote criticizing the efforts of the two eminent scientists to demolish Marconi's claims. Here we consider only Lodge's examination of Marconi's work, because it is a good example of what may happen when the process of examination for novelty is left undefined and in the hands of a self-interested party.

Oliver Lodge (1851–1940) held the chair of physics at University College, Liverpool from 1881 to 1900. He was then chosen to be the first principal of the new University of Birmingham, a position he held until 1920. He was thus asked to consider Marconi's work at a time when he should have felt he was at the peak of his career. He was knighted in 1902. In his report on Marconi's patents, Lodge began by claiming that a demonstration he himself had given at the Royal Institution in June 1894 had 'started the work of Righi in Italy, of Popoff in Russia, of Capt. Jackson in England and Bose in India'. The demonstration he referred to was certainly a demonstration of 'wireless' communication, from one end of the rostrum to the other, but Lodge went on to say that he 'did not pursue the matter' because 'he was unaware that there would be any demand for this kind of telegraphy' (PRO: ADM116/570; Jolly (1972), 88). He went on to fill twenty-four sides of foolscap with bitter complaints about Marconi and Preece stealing his ideas, and ended with the comment: 'What Marconi can righteously claim is that he has made the coherer work dependably and give good signals in ordinary Morse code, and that he has extended the method over remarkably great distances.'

This example of how not to have a patent examined should be borne in mind when we see, in Chapter 6, how a fairly well-defined system of examination did evolve by 1907. For the end of the story about Professors Lodge and Thompson (the latter comes over as an even sadder figure than Lodge) the reader should turn to Jolly's excellent presentation of the matter, of Captain Jackson's recognition of Marconi's work, and of the key position that the new Marconi Company built up in only a few years.

5.5   A Technical Revolution in the Air

The second technical revolution to be considered in this chapter, which again involves the offer of a secret to the British government, concerns the development of the aeroplane. There are many common features in the development of radio by Marconi and the development of flight by the Wright brothers, Orville (1871–1948) and Wilbur (1867–1912). There had been several previous demonstrations of powered flight, carrying a person, over very short distances, using steam and petrol engines, just as there had been many demonstrations of how electromagnetic waves could be generated and then detected, from one side of a lecture room to the other. What Marconi and the Wrights did was to put together hardware that worked. Like Marconi, the Wright brothers were systems engineers. They combined the development of a light and powerful air-cooled petrol engine with a deep understanding of the control surfaces that an air pilot must use in order to keep an aircraft stable and flying in the direction and at the height he intends.

The Wright brothers did their work near Dayton, Ohio. By 1905 they were making flights of over thirty minutes' duration and over distances of some twenty miles. 'The utmost secrecy, however, was maintained concerning their experiments, and in consequence their achievements were regarded at the time with doubt and suspicion' (*EB*11, 10 at 518).

The reason for all the secrecy becomes clear when we read a 'very confidential' report to the British War Office, dated 17 August 1906, written by Lieutenant-Colonel Count Edward Gleichen (PRO: WO32/8595), a military attaché to the British ambassador to the USA at the time. He went to Dayton to meet the Wright brothers, at their request, and to see their work. It is interesting to note that Andrew, in his book on the British secret service, identifies Gleichen as assistant director of military operations and intelligence from 1907 to 1911 and virtually the founder of what is now MI6 (Andrew (1985), 21–2, 26–7, 32). Gleichen wrote with great enthusiasm about what he had seen at Dayton: the Wrights had a one-man plane that could fly at 40 m.p.h., for which they wanted $100,000, plus a further $100,000 for the design theory and all the details of construction. He reported that 'they refuse to sell to anyone except Governments for military purposes', and that so far the United States government had not taken up their offer. On the patent question, the Wrights had no patents, and did not plan to apply for any, because the idea behind their aircraft was 'unpatentable, depending as it does not on a particular mechanism, but on a development of mathematics and physics in an unexpected direction'.

Gleichen concluded with an enthusiastic recommendation that the British government should strike a bargain with the Wrights. He believed that the price could be brought down a little. This was not well received in London. The superintendent of the Balloon Factory poured cold water on the whole project (PRO: WO32/8595), presumably just as his opposite number in the USA had done. Nothing came of the matter and, as the Wrights' biographers (Kelly (1943); Howard (1988); Crouch (1989)) tell us, the idea of attempting to sell secrets to powerful governments was soon abandoned by the Wrights. They realized that the control mechanisms and the design of the control surfaces they used could be the subject of a very strong patent (Howard (1988), ch. 38). The way forward was publicly to demonstrate their remarkable achievements, which they did with great success at Le Mans in 1909.

5.6   *Fathering the Unthinkable*

In this chapter we have looked at two cases where inventors directed their creative work towards a warlike purpose, in the hope of winning patronage from the state. It seems that the use to which their new ideas might have been put was of little concern to either Marconi or the Wrights. Their hope may simply have been to get on with their work, which they were clearly absorbed by, protected from worry about where the funds might come from. The atmosphere of secrecy that surrounds this kind of military research and development may also protect the people concerned from the nuisance of having to explain clearly what they are up to.

Neither Marconi nor the Wright brothers succeeded in their attempt to get this kind of patronage. The development of their ideas had to continue in a blaze of publicity, and there was no problem about financial support because their ideas were outstandingly good and could be applied to fulfil urgent practical needs. Nevertheless, there is an important problem here, which is being looked at by many authors today. How many important innovations, important in that our whole environment or way of living may be changed, are brought about by people who just get taken over by their fascination, and complete absorption, in some hardware problem? Brian Easlea's (1983) *Fathering the Unthinkable* may be the strongest critique of modern technology along these lines. Easlea finds the seeds of some of the worrying aspects of today's technologies back in the seventeenth century: a point he has made with considerable force in two other works (1980, 1981). Another author who has looked at this problem is Heims (1980), in his biography of John von Neumann and Norbert Wiener. These two men were both deeply involved in the development of weapons, but while von Neumann comes over as being unable to think of anything other than destruction, Wiener was clearly hoping to get away from such work as soon as possible. Both, however, had an obsession with hardware. Heims has an interesting quotation at the beginning of his Chapter 6 which tells us that Albert Einstein, for one, was well aware of the dangers and the origin of this kind of obsession. Recalling his first encounter with a book of verse by Virgil, Einstein wrote, 'The book shows me clearly what I fled from when I sold myself body and soul to science—the flight from the I and the WE to the IT.'

From this point of view, it is interesting to look back at Marconi and the Wright brothers. Were they flying from the I and the We, perhaps? As far as the Wrights are concerned, their biographers paint a picture of total hardware obsession: the two men worked only on their aircraft. There were no wives, no children, no friends even. Marconi seems very different, at first sight, but his enthusiasm for the opposite sex (Jolly (1972), 83, 147) belonged to the times in his life when he was separated from his hardware by travel. He seemed to be incapable of boarding a transatlantic liner without getting engaged to some young lady once the ship was well under way. When he was older, his affairs became very complicated (ibid. 244), but it was clear that he was then no longer interested in technical problems, which he left to the able young engineers he had gathered into his flourishing enterprise.

6

Introducing the Examiners

6.1 A Question in the House

Secret patents got off to a good start in the twentieth century when a question on them was asked in the House of Commons on 22 April 1901. William Redmond, MP for East County Clare, asked the Secretary of State for War to comment on the fact that two academics, who were also consultants to the War Office, had just applied for patents, in their own names, on improvements to detonators and explosives. William Redmond (1861–1917) was the younger brother of John Redmond (1851–1918), the leader of the Irish Nationalists at Westminster. His question on patents was the kind of question his party used, with good effect, continually to harass the government, at the time a radical Tory administration under the leadership of the Marquess of Salisbury and already embarrassed by its inability to bring the war in South Africa to an end. The question implied that some kind of corruption might be taking place, for the lay person, knowing that patents, like books, attract royalties for their authors, and that royalties by their very name must be of some consequence, would assume that great sums of money were involved. The Secretary of State had to give a full answer to the insinuation, and for the first time in Parliament some reasons were given for the policy on secret patents.

The two academics involved in the matter were Sir William Roberts (1843–1902), who was a professor of metallurgy at the Royal School of Mines, and Sir William Crookes (1832–1919), one of the most outstanding physical chemists of the time. They were both members of the Explosives Committee which the War Office had organized, under the chairmanship of Lord Rayleigh (1842–1919), to co-ordinate research and development in the United Kingdom and advise generally on explosive problems. The two patents concerned were BPN 5967 of 1901, entitled 'Detonators', to Sir William C. Roberts, and BPN 6513 of 1901, entitled 'Nitro-explosives', to Sir William Crookes. Neither is found in the collections of printed specifications, and the reason for this becomes clear when we refer to the *Journal* of the Patent Office. Both patents appear in the lists of complete specifications that have been accepted, but immediately after the title the entry states: 'Secret document under Section 44 of the Patents, Designs and Trade Marks Act, 1883' (*IOJ(P)* 677 at 1649; 682 at 117).

So what did the Secretary of State for War, St John Brodrick, who was soon to succeed his father and become the ninth Viscount Midleton, tell the House of Commons about the secret patents? He explained that both patents had been taken out

with my authority. The specifications were prepared by the patent expert at the War Office, and have been assigned to the Secretary of State for War . . . and the specifications are kept secret. . . . The only reason why patents have been taken out is that the Committee [Lord Rayleigh's] may not be debarred by some subsequent inventor from making use of their own results. It is obvious that, unless the Government directs either the publication or the patenting of such discoveries as they are made, this danger cannot be avoided. The Committee are studiously careful to avoid everything approaching to appropriation of discoveries communicated to them by inventors (H4, 92 at 905–6).

The Secretary of State's answer does not solve the persistent problem of how to recognize a specification that should be kept secret, or that corresponded to one that was already secret. There was still no examination of the technical content of patent applications at this time. Examination was being planned, however, as we shall see when we look at a report from a committee set up by the Board of Trade which had been looking at the Patent Acts during the summer of the previous year, 1900.

6.2   The Committee of the Board of Trade

'The Committee of the Board of Trade to inquire into the Working of the Patent Acts' held its first meeting on 12 June 1900. It was a small committee and well equipped. The chairman was Sir Edward Fry (1827–1918), one of England's most distinguished Chancery judges and Lord Justice of Appeal from 1883 to 1892. In retirement he had been chairman of many government commissions. Two members of the government, both distinguished in the legal profession, were on the committee: Lord Alverstone (1842–1915), the Master of the Rolls, and Sir Edward Carson

(1854–1935), the Solicitor-General. Another member waś John Fletcher Moulton (1844–1921), considered by many to be unrivalled at the patent Bar. Alverstone, Fry, and Moulton dominated the proceedings, and the minutes of evidence (BPP 1901 (530), xxiii. 611) are a valuable discussion on how the patent system operated at the time, particularly when the committee called their first witness, C. N. Dalton, then comptroller of the Patent Office.

C. N. Dalton (1842–1920) was the son of a country parson, attended a local grammar school, and then went to Trinity College, Cambridge, where he graduated in classics. A barrister of the Inner Temple by 1871, he had joined the Civil Service in 1873 and had had wide experience in many departments. He proved to be an outstanding head of the Patent Office for the final years of his career (1897–1909), seeing it through the difficult time during which technical examination of specifications was first introduced, and then made obligatory by statute. In his evidence before the committee, Dalton first outlined the way in which patents were processed and then began to talk about the problem of technical examination. He explained that the Act of 1883 required only that the Patent Office examine the application to ensure that three conditions were satisfied. The first was that the invention had to be described clearly. Secondly, the documents the inventor had submitted were checked to see that they had been prepared in the prescribed manner. Finally, the title the inventor had used was checked to see that it was sufficient and corresponded to the text.

That was all there was to examination in 1900, as far as the patent statutes were concerned. Dalton reminded the committee, however, that there were other statutes. The patent application could not be allowed if it was 'contrary to law or morality', as he put it; for example, an application for a patent mantrap could not be allowed. Mantraps were 'mechanical devices for catching poachers and trepassers' (*EB*11, 17 at 607) which had been widely used by the landowning classes in England in earlier times, but were now restricted by an Act of 1827. Another category of patent applications that would not do, Dalton explained, were 'articles apparently intended for sale in Holywell Street, such as quack doctors' appliances'. Holywell Street, demolished in 1905 when the Aldwych was built, was described by Walford as having 'gained a notoriety for the sale of books and prints of an immoral class' (1987, p. 34).

In Section 3.3 it was noted that between 1852 and 1883 a provisional specification may be found, among the printed specifications, that is not followed by a complete specification. This may mean that we have found a secret patent. Dalton's evidence confirmed that after 1883 this was no longer true: 'Since 1883 we have not printed any provisional specification which is abandoned. They are secret documents.' Dalton spoke at length on how the Patent Office was preparing for the introduction of examination of the technical content of specifications. This involved the preparation and printing of abridgements, and of detailed indexes and classifications. The work had begun in 1889, which was why the title of the *Journal* was changed in that year. After the 1883 Act, the old *Commissioners of Patents' Journal* became *The Official Journal of the Patent Office*. In 1889, however, when the abridgements began to be printed, nearly always including a diagram to make clear what the patent involved, the title was changed to *The Illustrated Official Journal (Patents)*, which it remained until 1931. By then the number of patents had grown so large that it was no longer possible to publish one week's abridgements, along with all the administrative detail that was needed, in one manageable issue of the *Journal*. The abridgements were thus split up into forty separate subject-groups and published separately. The journal became *The Offical Journal (Patents)*, and the title remains today.

All this work, from 1889 to 1900, had been done on the initiative of the Patent Office, and was intended to help inventors. By using the indexes and abridgements an inventor should have been able to avoid putting in an application for a patent when the idea had already been patented. A clearly defined procedure of examination was evolving that would answer one of the main aims that the Board of Trade committee of 1900 sought: to find a method of weeding out patent applications that repeated old ideas. There was no point in making the question a matter of opinion, even the opinion of 'men of scientific eminence', as we saw in Chapter 5.

As Harding (1953, p. 36) makes clear in his brief but valuable history of the Patent Office, published to celebrate its centenary, the committee was sitting at a time when the abridgements of past patent specifications, and the indexes and classification systems for them, had grown large enough to represent a database that could be used to answer a well-defined question: did a new patent application correspond to any previous ones? If it did, the new application could be compared with the old specifications and any duplication drawn to the inventor's attention. In 1900 the Patent Office could only draw the inventor's attention to the fact that he was attempting to patent an old idea. If he still wanted to go ahead, he had the right to do so. The committee's report (BPP 1901 (506), xxiii. 599) precipitated the preparation of a short bill to amend the patent law so that the Patent Office would be obliged to examine all new patent applications. An even more important reform proposed by the committee was also included in the bill which compelled people to work, or to allow others to work, their patents, instead of allowing them to use the patent to stop others working it. The bill became the Patent Law Amendment Act of 1902 (2 Edw. VII, c. 34).

6.3   The Act of 1902

The new bill was introduced to the House of Commons on 10 February 1902 by the President of the Board of Trade, Gerald Balfour, in Lord Salisbury's Conservative administration. At its second reading there was a long debate (H4, 110 at 852–79), but this was concerned mainly with the compulsory working of patents that the bill proposed. On the question of examination, one MP said he thought the idea 'a most extraordinary change in the existing law', and asked how the Patent Office was supposed to look through the past fifty years of old patent specifications every time they got a new patent application. The question was answered very effectively by Sir William Houldsworth, who had been a member of the committee of the Board of Trade. He explained to the House how the abridgements and classified indexes could be used (H4, 110 at 859). The bill went forward smoothly, with very little change, and received royal assent on 18 December 1902.

The Act of 1902 required the examiners at the Patent Office to continue to check on the three points required by the 1883 Act (see Section 6.2), and then to 'make a further investigation for the purpose of ascertaining whether the invention claimed had been wholly or in part claimed or described in any specification (other than a provisional specification not followed by a complete specification) published before the date of the application'. If the examiners found such a prior claim or description, the applicant was to be informed, and allowed to amend his application. The fact

that examination excluded 'provisional specification[s] not followed
by a complete specification' is interesting. These could only be
specifications published before 1883 and would have included, as
we saw in Section 3.3, some old secret patents. By 1902 it may
safely be assumed that these were secrets no longer. In any case,
the extra work put upon the Patent Office by the Act of 1902
meant that only the patents that had been sealed were being
abridged and indexed. There was still much work to be done before
there could be any hope of an up-to-date database being available. The detection of interference between patent applications
that were only a few weeks apart was to be left to the future. This
is clear from a report that C. N. Dalton submitted to the Board of
Trade in October 1905 (PRO: BT209/4). Holidays for the staff at
the Patent Office were being curtailed, he wrote, and they were
being asked to work overtime. The new system was, however,
working well, with 'little friction' between officials and inventors.
However, evidence of some friction between the Patent Office,
and the War Office and the Admiralty, was beginning to emerge
at this time.

6.4   The Acts Conflict

In Section 4.6 we saw how a conference was held at the War
Office, in 1891, where representatives of several government departments discussed the working of the 1883 Act. This clearly set
a precedent, for in the twentieth century, interdepartmental conferences or committees on patent matters became regular events.
There was one in 1906 but, unfortunately, the records have not
survived. We know about it only from references in later records.

A file in the Public Record Office marked 'Offical Secrets Act,
1920' (PRO: BT209/170), which was opened to the public in 1977,
refers to a contribution that C. N. Dalton made to the discussions
of an interdepartmental committee that met in 1906. Sir Cornelius
Dalton, as he was correctly referred to in these later papers of
1921, was reported to have said:

I am unable myself to endorse the proposal to require the Comptroller
(1) to divulge to the War Office or the Admiralty, as the case may be, the
content of Specifications prior to their acceptance if he considers them
anticipated by a secret patent; and (2) to refuse to accept specifications in
such cases without the consent of the War Office or Admiralty.

The person who was reminding the Board of Trade, in January 1921, about the 1906 meeting was A. J. Martin, the assistant comptroller of the Patent Office. He was doing so because the Air Ministry, founded in 1918, had made a complaint about what they considered to be a very serious leak of information concerning their latest fighting-machine. (We shall look at this case in detail at the end of the chapter.) A leak of an official secret would have involved the Offical Secrets Act. There had been two new Acts since that of 1889 (see Section 4.7), and these were the Acts of 1911 (1 & 2 Geo. V, c. 28) and 1920 (10 & 11 Geo, V, c. 75), the latter being an amending Act. As Rosamund Thomas makes clear (1991, pp. 5–24), these two Acts were concerned with better definitions of offences and of procedures for obtaining evidence. The rules for patents were unchanged: once an inventor filed a specification it became an official document and could easily be promoted to the status of an official secret.

The file continues with a report written by Martin on an inter-departmental conference he attended in December 1921 at the Admiralty. Representatives from the War Office, the Admiralty, the Air Ministry, the Treasury solicitor's office, the public prosecutor's office, and the Board of Trade (the latter being Martin himself) were present. Clearly, the same proposal that Dalton had had to reply to in 1906 came up again in 1921. 'I was invited to elaborate the objections of the Board of Trade', Martin reported, and he did so as follows:

if the two Acts conflicted, that is to say, the Offical Secrets Act which said it was an offence to publish certain matters, and the Patents Act, which imposed the statutory duty upon the Comptroller of publishing all accepted specifications, it was doubtful whether the Comptroller could be said to be guilty of an offence when he was merely carrying out a statutory duty. If the two Acts did conflict it was the fault of Parliament. . . . the sooner the Official Secrets Act was amended the better. . . . I pointed out that to harass an inventor or to frighten him was not the way to encourage invention . . . any inventor was only too anxious to get his invention taken up by the Fighting Departments, and that if an inventor was anxious to disclose the invention to a Foreign State no power on earth could prevent him doing so.

This bitter argument between the fighting departments and the Patent Office seems to have been going on from at least 1906 until the end of 1921. Between 1906 and 1921, however, there had been a new Patent Act, that of 1907, and a major war.

6.5   The Patent Act of 1907

After the general election of 1905 a Liberal administration took over from the Tories, who had been in power for the past ten years, and the new President of the Board of Trade was David Lloyd George (1863–1915). It was his turn to introduce a new Patents and Designs Bill to the House of Commons on 19 March 1907 (H4, 171 at 683–6). There was some urgency about patent law reform, Lloyd George explained, because the present law was being used 'to discourage the British inventor and to destroy many British industries'. To stop the alleged abuse, the new bill simplified and cheapened the compulsory licence appeal system, simplified appeals for revocation on grounds of inadequate working in the United Kingdom, made it much more difficult to patent a process of chemical synthesis that the patentee had not yet got to work properly, and, finally, tried to make it illegal for restrictive conditions to be included in patent lease agreements. This last item of reform was soon abandoned because people in a free society must be free to make any kind of private contract between themselves. That is, after all, what business is all about. The new bill also brought the system of examination, defined by the Act of 1902, to bear on the acceptance of a specification. If the inventor's application was anticipated by a previous application it could be refused.

During the second reading of the bill (H4, 172 at 1012–56) it became clear that the German chemical industry had precipitated much of the need for patent law reform. The progress of the bill became complicated when a consolidation bill was introduced in parallel, on 18 April 1907, to bring together the bits and pieces of the many Patent Acts that now lay behind it, but at no stage was the question of secret patents mentioned. Both bills received royal assent on 28 August 1907. The important one for our purposes is the Consolidation Act, which is the Patents and Designs Act 1907 (7 Edw. VII, c. 29).

Section 30 of the 1907 Act, which deals with secret patents, is interesting because it appears, at first glance, simply to repeat section 44 of the previous Act, of 1883, with the addition of the words 'or the Admiralty' after every mention of the Secretary of State for War. At the very end of section 30 of the Act of 1907, however, there is a completely new subsection, subsection 13, in which 'or the Admiralty' becomes 'and the Admiralty'. This reads as follows:

Rules may be made under this Act, after consultation with the Secretary of State and the Admiralty, for the purpose of ensuring secrecy with respect to patents to which this section applies, and those rules may modify any of the provisions of this Act in their application to such patents as aforesaid so far as may appear necessary for the purpose aforesaid.

The origin of the new subsection may be a 'Secret Patents Committee' which is mentioned in some papers dealing with the preparation of the two bills of 1907 (PRO: BT209/457). When the wording of subsection 13 was discussed, a memorandum noted that the intention was 'to meet the views of the Admiralty and War Office and carry out such of the recommendations of the Secret Patents Committee as appear free from objection'. One person who certainly knew what the objectionable recommendations, if any, were was C. N. Dalton, the Patent Office comptroller. In a letter dated 21 January 1907 he wrote, 'I left with him a copy of the report of the Secret Patents Committee.' Unfortunately a copy of the report has not been left in the file with Dalton's letter (PRO: BT209/457).

To the military men who sat on the Secret Patents Committee, subsection 13 may have appeared to put considerable power into their hands. In fact, subsection 13 is simply an example of the details of putting legislation into effect being delegated to the people actually concerned with the work, in this case the comptroller and his staff. This is a well-established practice (Mackenzie (1968), ch. 11). Many sections of the various Patent Acts allow the comptroller to make rules, and these are published from time to time as the *Patent Rules*. The last time secret patents appeared explicitly in the *Patent Rules*, as rules 106 to 108, was in the July 1939 printing. What happened after that we shall see in Chapter 9.

6.6   The Great War

The war of 1914 to 1918 did not involve the kind of technical revolutions that were to take place during the Second World War. The Great War was a war of almost personal combat. What might be termed technically advanced weapons, like machine-guns, tanks, poison gas, and aircraft, were used, but they had been around for some time and were only developed, or improved, during the war. For this reason we shall not be concerned with much technical detail in the rest of this chapter, but concentrate instead on the political battle between the Patent Office and the fighting departments. The argument was all about the conflict that was seen to exist between official secrets on the one hand, and the confidentiality of an inventor's patent application on the other.

The first shots in this battle were arguably fired by King George V himself. On 14 August 1914, a few days after the outbreak of hostilities, 'His Majesty was pleased to make Regulations' by means of an Order in Council at Buckingham Palace (PRO: AVIA8/10). These regulations, often referred to by the acronym DORA, because they are made under the delegation of the many Defence of the Realm Acts, gave the government the emergency powers thought necessary in time of war. Regulation 18b is the one of importance in the context of this book.

Regulation 18b concerns the comptroller of patents, designs, and trade marks, and states that if he 'is satisfied that the publication of the invention or design [described in an application for a patent] might be detrimental to the public safety or the defence of the Realm', he can prohibit the publication or communication of the invention in any way, and prohibit a patent application for it in any other country. Applying for a patent in a foreign country without first applying in the United Kingdom was now forbidden for all residents of the United Kingdom.

The effect of Regulation 18b was that officials from the Ministry of Munitions were to be found in the Patent Office during the Great War, checking through the incoming patent applications for those that might be of interest. For example, Colonel Spencer, who was the representative of the Ministry of Munitions during the early years of the war, reported on his work on 16 December 1916. A quotation from his report (PRO: BT209/190) makes it clear that his procedure was to read the incoming applications and, when he considered one to be of interest, he would write to the inventor asking for a copy of the application, in confidence, for the War Office or the Admiralty. He reported that he had had no problems in getting the inventors to co-operate.

Letters written at the time by the comptroller, who was now W. T. Franks, tell us that the Colonel's procedure had been laid down by the Patent Office. Franks wrote: 'The practice of this Office has always been as follows:—That unaccepted specifications filed on applications for patents . . . are considered and treated as confidential documents and have never been disclosed to any person or to any other Government Department without the consent of the applicant or his agent' (PRO: BT209/190). This was written on 19 July 1918, so it is clear that the Patent Office upheld the confidentiality required by the Patent Acts throughout the Great War. They did not find this easy, however. A letter from the comptroller to the chairman of the Air Inventions Committee, part of the new Air Ministry that was set up in 1918, pointed out that Regulation 18b did not authorize them to have any part in advising the Patent Office on questions covered by the regulation, simply because the regulation did not mention them. They should rectify this, the comptroller wrote. Later he wrote again, on 24 April 1918, 'I should also be glad to be informed of the names of the Officers deputed to inspect specifications at this Office and the subjects with which they will deal' (PRO: AVIA8/10). The Air Ministry put in four names for this work, and the comptroller protested that the Ministry of Munitions were covering the problem with only one officer, presumably Colonel Spencer. The Air Ministry insisted, and Franks replied in May 1918, 'I cannot resist the Air Ministry.' By giving way like this in unimportant matters, the comptroller was able to concentrate on the serious cases.

One serious case that we have a record of concerned Professor Frederick Soddy (1877–1956) of Aberdeen. He is particularly remembered for his work on isotopes, for which he received the Nobel prize for chemistry in 1921. Soddy had filed an application for a patent, entitled 'A method of stripping the illuminants from and of purifying coal gas by means of charcoal', on 8 May 1918. For some reason Lord Moulton (the John Fletcher Moulton of Section 6.2), who was director-general of explosive supplies at the Ministry of Munitions during the war, decided to make Soddy's patent a test case: would the Patent Office send a copy of Soddy's application to Lord Moulton without asking Professor Soddy first?

The exchanges in this particular battle, between Lord Moulton and the comptroller, W. T. Franks, went as follows (PRO: BT209/190). At first Lord Moulton raised the question generally and wrote to the comptroller on 23 July 1918, 'I think that the representatives of the various Ministries . . . have undoubtedly the right to see the applications which concern the work of their Ministry without obtaining the permission of the applicants.' He based this opinion—and we must remember that he was an outstanding barrister specializing in patent law—on section 29 of the Act of 1907. This was virtually identical to section 27 of the Act of 1883 (quoted in Section 4.5), which gave the Crown the right to use any invention and then, either 'before or after the use thereof', agree on terms. The comptroller wisely made no comment.

Lord Moulton's next move was to instruct his man at the ministry, one W. Gordon, to write to the Patent Office and request a copy of Soddy's patent application. This was on 17 August. The comptroller got his man to reply that this could not be done 'without the authority of the applicant'. Lord Moulton himself then wrote, no longer to 'Dear Mr Temple Franks' but to 'Dear Mr Controller' (*sic*), and stated, 'I must insist on the rights of the Crown being exercised.' The comptroller took his time to reply to that. After all, the Crown had rights only over patents: Professor Soddy had not yet got one. On 19 September 1918 the comptroller answered that this was a matter of Patent Office policy and they could not 'undermine the confidence which I believe inventors at present have as regards our complete impartiality and the protection which we afford to them against the actions of other government offices'. Lord Moulton had to admit defeat. He replied within a few days: 'I do this out of respect for your wishes and not in any way because I have the slightest doubt of the right of the representatives of the Crown to see the Provisional Specifications.'

This was not the end of the story, however, because it is clear from the records that Professor Soddy had been contacted by the comptroller and they had met on 18 September. The next day, when Franks was writing to Moulton, Soddy wrote to Franks to tell him that he had decided to write to Moulton himself and offer to come and show him the patent specification, and discuss it, but no copies would be handed over. On receiving this news, Lord Moulton got another of his men, one A. Bazine, to reply that his lordship felt 'that any information required by him should perhaps be obtained through the official channels'.

Professor Soddy was very upset by all this. Staying at the Langham Hotel during his visit to London, he wrote to the comptroller that he thought he had done all he could to be co-operative and that he considered 'that the treatment to which I have been subjected by the Explosives Department . . . to be manifestly and flagrantly unfair'. His patent was published in the normal way in June 1919 (BPN 125253).

6.7   Peace

Peace and the celebration of victory may have come to the United Kingdom in November 1918, but strife at the Patent Office was to continue for at least a few years. The interdepartmental conference that took place in December 1921, referred to in Section 6.4, had been preceded by a rather unpleasant exchange of letters between the Patent Office and the fighting departments. The senior service fired the first shot with a letter from the Admiralty, dated 20 January 1921. They wanted to make the relationship between the new Official Secrets Act of 1920 and the existing patent law quite clear:

The opinion of the Director of Public Prosecutions was obtained . . . and, resulting from his advice, the definition of 'Munitions of War' in the new Official Secrets Act has been worded in such a way as to bring within the scope of the definition an entirely new war-like invention (whether actually existing or only proposed) produced by the brain of an inventor. . . . to make the new provisions effective . . . the Comptroller should have power, where application is made for the grant of a patent in respect of 'Munitions of War', to Communicate the application, confidentially, in good time before publication, to the appropriate fighting Department, who should then have power to take some action which would effectively prevent publication if in the opinion of the Department such publication would be prejudicial to the safety or interest of the State (PRO: BT209/ 170).

The Patent Office answered this on 1 February with a straightforward statement that the patent law simply made such a breach of confidentiality out of the question. Peace reigned for a few weeks, and then letters arrived at the Patent Office from the War Office on 23 March, and from the Air Ministry on 30 March, which virtually repeated the statement of 20 January from the Admiralty. The Patent Office simply repeated their statement of the patent law. On 7 July 1921 a strong letter from the Admiralty arrived at the Patent Office. It demanded a meeting to discuss these problems and begin the process of amending the patent law. The Board of Trade agreed and the interdepartmental conference was set up to meet on 9 December.

A. J. Martin's report back to the Board of Trade on the December conference was quoted above in Section 6.4. The only concession that the fighting departments managed to get out of the Patent

Office as a result of the conference was that they agreed to consider issuing a notice to inventors warning them that they should think about the problems that might arise when their inventions touched upon the field of munitions of war. Several months passed, and many letters were exchanged, while the exact wording of the notice was thrashed out. The 'Official Notice to Inventors' was finally agreed in form, and it was first printed in the *Journal* on 28 June 1922. It ran as follows:

Notice to Inventors

The attention of applicants for patents is drawn to the desirability of avoiding publication of inventions in cases where the invention relates to Munitions of War as defined in the Official Secrets Acts, 1911 and 1920.

In such cases, after lodging an application at the Patent Office and thus obtaining protection, the inventor is advised to submit the details of his invention confidentially to the departments concerned, i.e., Admiralty, War Office, or Air Ministry, in good time before publication takes place in order that if considered necessary by such departments, steps may be taken for the invention, and any patent to be granted thereon, to be kept secret, under the provisions of Section 30 of the Patents and Designs Acts, 1907 and 1919, on such terms as may be arranged (*IOJ(P)* 1745 at 961).

Such a notice, suitably brought up to date, has appeared on the first page of every issue of the *Journal* since its first appearance over seventy years ago. Today it is somewhat longer and inventors are encouraged to telephone the Patent Office should they feel the need. Nevertheless, in 1922, and even now, some inventors may not see the *Journal*. There may even be inventors who are unaware that the *Journal* exists. This worried the Admiralty back in 1922, and they asked that every applicant for a patent be sent an individual copy of the notice. The Patent Office ordered 10,000 copies to be printed (PRO: BT209/170).

The assistant comptroller of patents, A. J. Martin, thought all the fuss unnecessary. He noted in a memorandum of 16 November 1922 that:

The War Office and the Admiralty do not regard this question from the same point of view as we do. They are obsessed with the idea of the desirability of being informed of all inventions relating to munitions of war at the earliest possible moment and in order to meet their views we have undertaken to furnish them with the addresses of all inventors who file applications for patents relating to munitions of war (PRO: BT209/ 170).

Did this mean that the Patent Office had capitulated? Not at all. The fighting departments realized that being given a list of addresses could well confuse the whole issue. They decided to look through the *Journal* themselves, checking the titles that inventors used to describe their patent applications, and then asking for the addresses.

After a number of false starts, one of the fighting departments at last found a patent, which had been applied for in May 1922 and had gone through the whole system smoothly to be sealed and published in November 1923, that they believed should have been kept secret. Here, surely, was the evidence that something must be done to change the patent law. The patent in question was BPN 206537.

Patent No. 206537 was to the aircraft manufacturers A. V. Roe and Company Limited. The Air Ministry protested to the Patent Office about this patent in July 1924 (PRO: BT209/170), but they had protested to A. V. Roe somewhat earlier, in February (PRO: AVIA8/17). The records show that they took some time over drafting their letter of protest, but it finally went off to A. V. Roe on 16 February, signed by the secretary to the Air Ministry, W. F. Nicholson. 'Secrecy can no longer be maintained', he wrote, 'with regard to the highly important question of the arrangement of armament', and one can see what he meant by looking at the diagram that went with the published specification of BPN 206537 (see Fig. 5). If a potential enemy would not have been alarmed by such a machine, the airmen who might have to fly in it surely would have been!

A. V. Roe answered promptly to say they would look into the matter, and came back with a full response on 26 February 1924. The drawing in the patent specification, they explained, was supposed to show only 'a plurality of intercommunicating decks', because that was all, in fact, that their patent claimed. The aircraft concerned, the *Aldershot*, was one of the first to allow people to move around inside the fuselage, taking up various positions to perform various tasks. This was the idea that A. V. Roe hoped to stake out for themselves in the intellectual property market. The draughtsman who had prepared the drawings for the patent

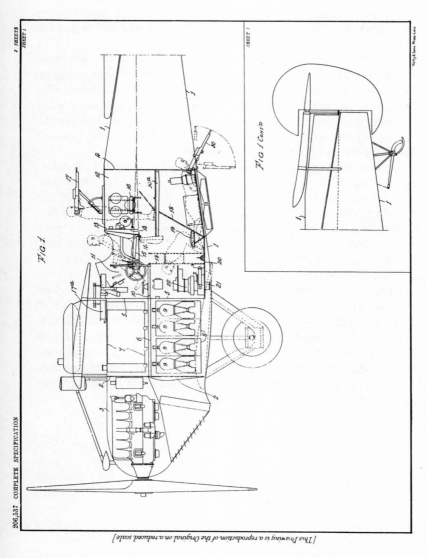

206,537   COMPLETE SPECIFICATION

[*This Drawing is a reproduction of the Original on a reduced scale*]

FIG. 5. Diagram from the specification of BPN 206537

application, they explained, was supposed to have deleted all the bombs, bomb-sights, and guns, leaving only the 'plurality of inter-communicating decks'. 'Plurality', it should perhaps be noted, is patentese, and readers of patent specifications will find it used a plurality of times.

When the Patent Office received the protest from the Air Ministry about BPN 206537, they first wrote to A. V. Roe's patent agents to see if they had any comments. This was in July 1924. The agents wrote back promptly to point out that A. V. Roe were government contractors and should, therefore, know all about the Official Secrets Acts (PRO: BT209/170)! The Patent Office passed this observation on to the Air Ministry.

The last word in the *Aldershot* affair should go to E. L. Pickles, who had been employed as an examiner at the Patent Office before the war, and seconded to the Air Ministry in 1918 (PRO: AVIA8/10). By 1924 Pickles had become an employee of the Air Ministry and was their expert on patent affairs. He wrote a report on the *Aldershot* case in which he reminded the Air Ministry how the War Office had, for many years, pressed the Patent Office to let them see pending patent applications 'so that steps can be taken with the applicant to have the patent made secret and so prevent publication'. He went on to say that the Patent Office had always refused to allow this and, in his opinion, they had done this on very good grounds. He concluded: 'I think in general we can rely on any inventor who has an invention of real military importance bringing it to the notice of the Department before publication. This can be stimulated by generous treatment of inventors in the matter of payment' (PRO: AVIA8/17).

7

Between the Wars

7.1 A Committee of the Privy Council

The recognition that something might be wrong in the way that British industry had been organizing itself had come quite early in the 1914–18 war. In July 1915 a government paper outlining what the new policy should be for supporting industrial research stated:

It is well known that many of our industries have since the outbreak of war suffered through our inability to produce at home certain articles and materials required in trade processes, the manufacture of which has become localized abroad, and particularly in Germany, because science has there been more thoroughly and effectively applied to the solution of scientific problems bearing on trade and industry and to the elaboration of economical and improved processes of manufacture (BPP 1914–16 (8005), l. 351).

To remedy this sad situation, the paper proposed that a committee of the Privy Council be set up to deal with expenditure of funds provided by Parliament and, secondly, that a small advisory council be formed, 'composed mainly of eminent scientific men and men actually engaged in industries dependent on scientific research'. This marked the beginning of the Department of Scientific and Industrial Research (DSIR), which was to administer the allocation of state funds for research to the universities, industry, and, in rare cases, individuals, for the next fifty years.

The first report from the committee of the Privy Council, in August 1916, suggests that little was being done in the way of government support for research. Grants of only £1,000 or so had been made (BPP 1916 (8336), viii. 469). By the time of the second report, income had improved, if not expenditure, because the government had set up 'The Million Fund for Trade Research Associations' (BPP 1917–18 (8718), xi. 531). The idea was to provide a fund of £1 million to be allocated to various branches of industry so that research laboratories could be set up to look at

the problems of that particular industry. The money allocated by
the DSIR had to be matched by the industry concerned.

A number of such research associations were set up, some of
which survive today, for example the Electrical Research Association and the Scientific Instruments Research Association. These
laboratories were small organizations, employing only a few people.
Even so, one might expect that the £1 million would have been
put to good use fairly soon, but the records show some reluctance
to spend. Interest rates were high at the time, and the DSIR had
problems stopping the 'Million Fund' from growing. By 1920 they
had got it down to £954,870. 12*s.* 6*d.* (BPP 1920 (905), xxv. 133).

7.2 Rewards for Inventors

Once the idea of the DSIR supporting scientific research in the
universities and in private industry had become well established,
the question of patents was soon brought up. When a group or an
individual, supported by a DSIR grant, came up with a patentable
idea, what should the procedure be and, most important of all,
who was to receive the income, if any, from the patent? The question brought about the setting-up of an interdepartmental committee 'to consider the methods of dealing with inventions made
by workers aided or maintained from public funds' (PRO: BT209/
267–73). The committee met between November 1920 and July
1921. Its report was published by HMSO early in 1922, after taking evidence from all the fighting departments, the Post Office,
private industry, and one trade union. The committee itself represented an equally wide range of interests: the Board of Trade, the
War Office, the Admiralty, the Air Ministry, the Medical Research
Council, the DSIR, the Post Office. Attending in person were the
editor of *Nature* and Sir Charles A. Parsons, FRS, who could represent private industry as he was chairman of the electrical company that bore his name.

The recommendations of the committee were, as would be expected from such a wide field of interests, rather vague and general. The best solution to these problems, they sensibly suggested,
was to leave each individual case to the head of department concerned. The documents that survive to give an account of how the
committee actually worked have some interesting features, however. For example, in a memorandum that circulated in the Board

of Trade, Percy Ashley, one of the assistant secretaries, pointed out that the DSIR 'has shown a disposition to patent every discovery that could be patented' (PRO: BT209/273). This had to be discouraged, he wrote; there were problems about the administrative costs patenting to excess caused, and, anyway, what was to be done with all the patents? They were coming from people, for example university staff, who had no wish to manufacture, and it followed that licensees had to be found if any income were to be made from these patents.

The comptroller of the Patent Office, W. T. Franks, did not agree with his colleague. He pointed out that many of the developments coming out of work supported by the DSIR were, as the committee's final report put it, 'of value for the preservation of health and life' (PRO: BT209/267 at 20), and it was important to stop other people obtaining a monopoly of such developments. This could be done by going through the procedure of taking out a patent, but only to the extent where the complete specification was published. If the applicant then never asked for the patent to be sealed, no patent would be issued, but the existence of the printed specification would stop any other person from obtaining a British patent for the same idea. Unfortunately this procedure ran into difficulties when foreign patents were involved.

7.3 The Disclosure of Colonel Clark

The Patent Office was represented on the interdepartmental committee by one of its assistant comptrollers: Colonel W. H. D. Clark. He was specifically asked, at one of the first meetings, to prepare a memorandum for the committee on the question of secret patents. The problem had come up quite naturally in the proceedings of the committee because the DSIR had, at the beginning of its history, supported work considered essential for the war effort, and there was no reason why it should not find itself supporting projects that might have defence applications now that peace was established.

Clark submitted a detailed memorandum entitled 'Secret Patents' (PRO: BT209/268 at CP15), dated 20 December 1920. He was clearly concerned that he might have been a bit too open, for he wrote that one only had to look at the *Patent Rules* (see Section 6.6) to see what the procedure for dealing with a secret patent was. He added that 'little information other than that afforded by the terms of these rules can be disclosed', but then went ahead and told his readers a great deal more. Secret patents, he explained, were handled at the Patent Office in just the same way as other patents, but secretly. The detailed work was done by 'the Comptroller's Private Secretary, the Special Examiner of Secret Patents, and one or two special assistant examiners, but are not communicated to any other member of the staff'. There was a register kept of all the secret patents, he explained but, as this itself was a secret document, 'no information as to the number of such patents can be disclosed'. As the very existence of a secret patent was suppressed, the Colonel pointed out that no one could oppose such a patent being granted or attack its validity. He wrote that this aspect of the system might lead to a secret patent being 'granted to a person other than the true and first inventor ... without any possibility of the fraud coming to the knowledge of the person aggrieved'. This was a surprising admission from someone so deeply involved in the system itself, and it is difficult to understand why Clark put this remark in.

He discussed the question of reassignment in his memorandum: 'When a secret patent is re-assigned to the inventor [because it is no longer thought necessary to keep it secret], the specification is accorded a serial number, is published, and is included in the search files of the Patent Office.' The mention of serial numbers brings up an important change in practice that took place in 1916. Before 1916 all British patent specifications were numbered according to the order of application in any year, starting afresh each year with No. 1. That is why they must be referred to by a number followed by the year of application. It is obvious that this system can cause problems when the specifications come to be bound, because some patents are sealed, and thus published, very quickly, while others may take some time. It was decided in 1916 that in future a cumulative numbering system would be adopted. The first specification published in 1916 was given the number 100,001, and this system continued until the Patents Act of 1977.

This change makes it much easier to identify a secret patent that has been declassified, as we would say today. The sign is a period of several years between the date of application and the date of publication. An early example of this is a patent to Lieutenant-Commander George Hazelton, RNVR, for a system of synchronizing the firing of guns on an aircraft so that they could be safely fired through the rotating propeller blades of the machine in flight. Hazelton's patent was made secret and assigned to the Admiralty when he first applied for it in 1918 (PRO: TS21/68; AVIA8/320). It was later published as BPN 162679 in 1921. Apart from this delay of a few years, there is no clue on the printed specification that there is anything special about the patent. The case is an interesting one, however, because, while the Admiralty declassified Hazelton's patent after only a few years, his new employers, the RAF, apparently believed that BPN 162679 was still secret in 1934 when it expired (PRO: AVIA8/320).

Clark brought up an interesting point in his memorandum about the effect that these delayed publications, of patents that were no longer secret, might have. The Patent Act of 1907 had made provision, in section 8, for cases where two or more patent applications might be made for the same idea at more or less the same time. It did not follow that the inventor who applied first got published first. During the two-month period that had to elapse between publication and sealing, it should have been possible, once the Patent Office was making examinations using up-to-the-minute data, to notice that two specifications had just been printed covering very similar ideas, and then check which one belonged to the 'true and first inventor', as the old Statute of Monopolies had put it so well in 1623 (see Section 2.3). For this reason, section 8 of the Act of 1907 made it possible for the examiners to look at specifications 'published subsequently to the application' and, wisely, did not say how subsequent this might be. Clark wrote that it did sometimes happen that 'the later patentee finds, after a lapse of years from the date at which his patent was sealed, that his invention was wholly anticipated by one which had been secretly patented'.

Clark gave no examples, and it seems very unlikely that such cases would have been allowed to arise. Once a patent is sealed, a court hearing is needed to overturn it and there is no sign of such a case involving a secret patent in the *UK Reports of Patent Cases* for the years 1908 to 1920, these being the only years when such a case could have arisen for Colonel Clark to write about in 1920. Again, it is difficult to understand why Clark brought up these worrying points. He concluded his two-page memorandum with the following: 'A secret patent, it will thus be seen, occupies an exceptional position, both in respect of its validity, and in respect of its effect on the validity of other patents—a position that can be justified only by the paramount necessity of safeguarding the safety of the Realm' (PRO: BT209/268 at CP15). The Colonel had recognized that the secret patent idea could lead to all kinds of complications. Secret patents were patents, only more so. This chapter continues with a look at three cases that illustrate the kind of difficulties that secret patents ran into between the two world wars.

7.4   The Case of the Autopilot

In the 1920s the most exciting area of technological development was flight. The United Kingdom government, for once, had recognized the importance of this area and by 1918 the Royal Aircraft Establishment (RAE) had been set up at Farnborough as a centre of research and development. It remains a major centre for aerospace research and development today. RAE can trace its origins back to 1878 when a centre for balloon equipment was set up at the Woolwich Arsenal. This became the Balloon Factory, at Aldershot, in 1892, the establishment that turned down the Wright brothers (see Chapter 5). The Balloon Factory moved to Farnborough in 1912, was renamed the Royal Aircraft Factory, and became RAE six years later.

RAE saw some of the earliest research and development work on inertial guidance systems. These systems make use of the fact that a gyroscope can sense any change in the direction that an aircraft is flying. It is very important that the pilot has some kind of instrumentation to give this information, especially at night or when flying in thick cloud, because very small, unnoticed, deviations from the desired course add up over time and can lead to serious consequences. People were working on the idea of inertial guidance all over the world. The Sperry Gyroscope Company was perhaps the leader in the field in the 1920s, and another group, often mentioned in the literature of the time, was the Société Anonyme des Établissement Marmonier Fils. The team on inertial guidance systems at RAE was led by P. A. Cooke and F. W. Meredith, and their contribution to the art was to concentrate on the stability problems that came up in such systems. Stability is a problem in inertial guidance systems because correcting the course of an aircraft by means of the control surfaces, using the error signal from the gyroscopes, means that at least two closed-loop control systems have been set up, one for bearing and one for elevation, which are not only coupled but also non-linear. For example, rate of turn is a very non-linear function of the angle at which the control surfaces may be set, and the forces on these control surfaces change in a very non-linear way.

The work at RAE resulted in four patents (PRO: AVIA8/209). These were all applied for provisionally on 18 July 1925, and sealed about eighteen months later. All four were kept secret. The reason for this was that the work looked as though it might lead to the development of a pilotless bombing aircraft, but it soon became clear that this was a long way in the future and that the simple autopilot that had been developed would be suitable only as a 'pilot assistor', as RAE called it. The system was reliable enough to fly the aircraft under very calm weather conditions, when the course was dead ahead at constant altitude. Such a system could therefore be valuable for reducing pilot fatigue during long flights. It was, RAE decided, just the thing for the new Imperial Airways Limited, the forerunner of today's British Airways, which had been set up, with considerable financial help from the British government, in March 1924.

The problem now was to get the four patents declassified, to get rid of their secret status. Once this had been done, patents could be taken out world-wide and commercial firms persuaded to enter into licensing agreements to manufacture the autopilot for sale to Imperial Airways, and to any of the other new airlines that were springing up all over the globe. The decision to do this was taken at the end of 1929, and it was obviously assumed that the declassification of the four patents, and reassignment to Cooke and Meredith, subject to some sensible agreement with the Air Ministry, would go ahead fairly quickly. With this in mind, RAE planned a press release and invited the *Illustrated London News* and the *Graphic* to write the story up as a description of a new invention which would reduce pilot fatigue. This was duly published in August 1930, and included an artist's impression of the flight deck of such an advanced airliner, showing two well-dressed airmen drinking coffee and smoking while the plane flew itself. An insert to the illustration showed the two gyroscopes sending hydraulic control signals to rudder, elevators, and ailerons (PRO: AVIA8/209).

Unfortunately, the patents had not been published before August 1930, when the illustrated article appeared in the popular press. In fact, due to unexpected administrative problems, the patents were not published until December 1931. The patents concerned are BPN 365186, 365187, 365188, and 365190. All the printed specifications show acceptance dates in late 1926 or early 1927 and then, in parentheses, the words 'but withheld from publication under Section 30 of the Patents and Designs Acts of 1907 to 1928'. This parenthetical remark is not always found when a specification is published that has, for a period, been kept secret. The four patents from RAE may be the first examples of its use.

The delay of well over a year between the press releases and the publication of the four specifications caused a great deal of worry for the Air Ministry. Had too much been disclosed in the press releases, so as to jeopardize the applications for patents abroad, when, if ever, these could be filed? Even more irritating was the fact that a firm, Smith's Instruments Limited, had been found, in August 1931, which was interested in having a licence agreement, but the patents were still secret and Smith's was very unhappy about entering into any agreement while the secret status persisted. It was then that the Air Ministry's expert on patent matters, E. L. Pickles, whom we met at the end of the last chapter, intervened and saw the declassification process through, along with an agreement to reassign the patent rights to Cooke and Meredith. The reassignment agreement gave the Air Ministry 45 per cent of the royalties received by the inventors. By July 1932 world-wide patents had been taken out.

After all the trouble it might be thought that the patents would have brought a good return. Unfortunately, the records show, the income was not sufficient to cover the cost of the foreign patents that were taken out (PRO: AVIA8/209).

7.5   The Boulton Paul Case

On 16 December 1936 the *Journal* of the Patent Office published its usual lists of applications for patents. For applications that had been made on 4 December the list included three from the Boulton Paul Aircraft Company, at Wolverhampton: two for 'Sighting mechanisms for guns on aircraft' and the third for 'Determining relative speed of target aircraft'. Just two weeks after these announcements in the *Journal*, a letter went off from the director of contracts at the Air Ministry to the Boulton Paul Company, asking them to send 'for confidential information and return copies of the Specifications filed at the Patent Office . . . in order that the Department may satisfy themselves that there is no objection to publication' (PRO: AVIA8/332). Here we see the procedure that was described in Section 6.8 at work. The Air Ministry was checking through the lists of patent applications that were published in the *Journal*, and then asking the inventors to send details, in confidence, of any ideas that looked interesting.

The Boulton Paul Company sent the specifications that the Air Ministry had asked for straight away, but they also wrote to say that they did so 'on the express understanding that we retain our privileged position as provisional Patentees who have made a confidential disclosure to you, and that such disclosure shall not *per se* render the contents of the said specifications subject matter for an official secret'.

The Air Ministry replied at length on 25 January 1937, saying that the two patent applications for sighting mechanisms 'should be kept secret in the interests of the State'. They also wrote to the Patent Office to say the same thing. A deed of assignment was made out by the Treasury solicitor in February 1937, and the two patents were sealed by August 1938. Both can be found today in the printed specifications of British patents as BPN 587429, 'Improvements in Mechanisms for Computing Corrections to Bullet Trajectories to be Applied to the Sights of Guns in Aircraft', and BPN 587431, 'Improved Means of Determining Corrections Required for the Sighting of Guns Carried by Aircraft'. Both specifications were published on 29 January 1947, more than ten years after the initial application, and both bear the note, after the date of acceptance: 'but withheld from publication under Section 30 of the Patents and Designs Acts, 1907 to 1942'.

The two Boulton Paul patents dealt with computing gun-sights. The computer was, of course, a mechanical one, and had to be fed with all the relevant data needed to calculate the trajectory of the bullet, fired from the aircraft with the computer on board, that was intended to hit the target aircraft held in the gun-sight. This was no simple calculation because it involved the air speed of both aircraft, their relative velocity, the air density, which might vary along the trajectory, the muzzle velocity of the bullet and all its aerodynamic properties, and so on. The calculation had to be made quickly and on-line, due to the input data changing all the time, and it involved operations like taking square roots and using trigonometric functions. All this had to be done with mechanical linkages and cams. There were no electronic computers in 1936.

From the records, the Boulton Paul case appears to be a straightforward example of a private company being asked to put some of its patent applications into the secret patent domain. Keeping secrets is very much like telling lies, however: one secret leads to another. This point comes up in the records very clearly concerning the third patent, BPN 587430, 'Means of Determining the Relative Speed of a Target Aircraft from another Aircraft for Gun Aiming Purposes'. The printed specification of the patent, as its serial number shows, was also withheld from publication until 1947, which is not unexpected because the specification refers to its two neighbours, BPN 587429 and 587431. It describes one of the key computing linkages that is used in the sighting mechanisms.

A minute written just before the file (PRO: AVIA8/332) on this case was closed, in 1946, noted that 'unfortunately', by some oversight, BPN 587430 was not declared secret and could have been published. It appears that the Patent Office treated this patent as though it were a secret patent without ever receiving the certificate they needed in order to do this. The case is even further confused when we note that BPN 587430 has a printed specification bearing 20 December 1945 as its date of publication. This date, more than two years earlier than that of its neighbours, BPN 587429 and 587431, is incompatible with its serial number.

7.6   The Case of Leo Szilard

The final secret patent case from between the wars to be considered in this chapter does not concern a government laboratory or a private company but a single individual, the physicist Leo Szilard (1894–1968). Szilard had intended to become a civil engineer like his father (Jungk (1958), 58), but his studies at the Technical University, Budapest were interrupted by the Great War. Having survived conscription into the army of the Austro-Hungarian monarchy, he continued to study engineering in Berlin once the war was over, but there were great opportunities offered to physics students in Berlin at the time, with men like Einstein, Nernst, von Laue, Planck, and many others teaching and leading research. This caused Szilard to change his field to physics.

Szilard belonged to a family with considerable wealth and did not need to worry about money. He worked in many of the famous institutes in Berlin during the 1920s, often for no salary. In 1931 he travelled widely in the USA, visiting many laboratories, before returning to Germany. In 1933 the Nazi take-over of political power forced Szilard to leave Germany, first for Vienna and then for London. Weart and Szilard (1978) quote Szilard's recollections of his beginnings as a refugee in London, when he lived at the Strand Palace Hotel: 'I had a little money saved up, enough perhaps for a year . . . I was in no hurry to look for a job.' To begin his scientific life in England, Szilard worked with T. A. Chalmers in the physics department of one of the teaching hospitals of the University of London. He was soon offered a fellowship by one of the Oxford colleges, which he accepted at half-pay, for he wished to spend six months of the year working in the USA. He was to move to the USA permanently when war broke out in 1939.

It was from the Clarendon Laboratory of the University of Oxford that Szilard wrote a remarkable letter to the director of scientific research at the Admiralty. He also got Professor F. A. Lindemann to write a letter of introduction for him, and both letters are reproduced in Szilard's collected works (Feld and Szilard (1972), 733–4). The director of scientific research was C. S. Wright (1887–1975). Later to become Sir Charles Wright, this outstanding Canadian scientist, who was a member of Scott's famous Antarctic expedition of 1910–13, will feature prominently in the next chapter. He was to read in Professor Lindemann's letter, of 26 February 1936, 'about a man working here [the Clarendon Laboratory] who had a patent he thought ought to be kept secret'. Lindemann, politician that he was, recommended nothing and nobody either way beyond saying that Szilard 'is a very good physicist' and, if he really wanted his patent kept secret, 'it is not going to cost the Government anything'.

Wright, familiar with Lindemann's style, probably turned his attention at once to Szilard's letter, in which he explained how he had filed a patent application that 'contains information which could be used in the construction of explosive bodies . . . very many thousand times more powerful than ordinary bombs'. Szilard

thought it 'very undesirable' to publish such information and understood that if he agreed to assign his patent to the Admiralty it
could become a secret patent. He made it quite clear that he
expected no payment of any kind, and that his only motive was to
try and ensure that such powerful bombs 'should be developed in
this country a few years ahead of certain other countries', Nazi
Germany clearly being in his mind. This interesting episode may
be the first attempt that Szilard made to sound the alarm about
nuclear weapons, a project that he took further when he composed the famous letter for Albert Einstein to send to President
Roosevelt in August 1939 (Feld and Szilard (1972), 94–6).

What happened to the patent application that Szilard hoped
would be kept secret in 1936? BPN 630726 has the same application reference number (19157/34) that Szilard used in his letter to
Wright. The first page of the printed specification is reproduced in
Fig. 6(*a*). This shows that the patent was indeed kept secret for
thirteen years, being withheld from publication until September
1949. The complete specification of BPN 630726 does describe
chain reactions and critical masses, concepts essential for understanding an atomic bomb, but such ideas were in fairly wide cir-
culation at the time, and far more is involved in making an atomic
bomb.

Finally, it is interesting to note an earlier patent that Szilard
applied for in 1934, which had been accepted and published just
a few weeks before he sent his letter to Wright. This is BPN
440023, and the first page of the specification is reproduced in Fig.
6(*b*). Comparing the headings of BPNs 440023 and 630726 shows
that Szilard must have decided to 'divide out' what he believed it
was safe to disclose about his ideas for 'the transmutation of chemical elements' and put all this into what became BPN 440023. He
then made every effort, as he explained in his letter to Wright, to
delay the publication of what became BPN 630726 until the Admiralty could issue a certificate of secrecy.

7.7 *Time for a Change*

In this chapter we have read about an unexpected disclosure from
the very heart of the secret patents section of the British Patent
Office, and then looked at three particular cases in which patents
were made secret. These three cases were by no means the only

PATENT SPECIFICATION

630,726

Application Date: June 28, 1934. No. 19157/34.
„ „ July 4, 1934. No. 19721/34.

One Complete Specification left (under Section 16 of the Patents and Designs Acts, 1907 to 1946): April 9, 1935.

Specification Accepted: March 30, 1936 (but withheld from publication under Section 30 of the Patent and Designs Acts 1907 to 1932)

Date of Publication: Sept. 28, 1949.

Index at acceptance : —**Class 39(iv)**, P(1:2:3x).

PROVISIONAL SPECIFICATION
No. 19157 A.D. 1934.

Improvements in or relating to the Transmutation of Chemical Elements

I, LEO SZILARD, a citizen of Germany and subject of Hungary, c/o Claremont Haynes & Co., of Vernon House, Bloomsbury Square, London, W.C.1, do hereby 5 declare the nature of this invention to be as follows:—

This invention has for its object the production of radio active bodies the storage of energy through the production 10 of such bodies and the liberation of nuclear energy for power production and other purposes through nuclear transmutation.

In accordance with the present inven-15 tion nuclear transmutation leading to the liberation of neutrons and of energy may be brought about by maintaining a chain reaction in which particles which carry no positive charge and the mass of which 20 is approximately equal to the proton mass or a multiple thereof form the links of the chain.

I shall call such particles in this specification "efficient particles."

25 A way of bringing about efficiently transmutation processes is to build up transmutation areas choosing the composition and the bulk of the material so as to make chain reactions efficient and 30 possible, the links of the chain being "efficient particles."

One example is the following. The chain transmutation contains an element C, and this element is so chosen that an 35 efficient particle x when reacting with C may produce an efficient particle y, and the efficient particle y when reacting with C may produce either an efficient particle x or another efficient particle which in its 40 turn is directly or indirectly when reacting with C capable of producing x. The bulk of the transmutation area, on the other hand, must be such that the linear dimensions of the area should sufficiently

[*Price 2/-*]

exceed the mean free path between two 45 successive transmutations within the chain. For long chains composed of, say, 100 links the linear dimensions must be about ten times the mean free path.

I shall call a chain reaction in which 50 two efficient particles of different mass number alternate a " doublet chain." An example for a doublet chain which is a neutron chain would be the following reaction, which might be set up in a mix-55 ture of a " neutron reducer element " (like lithium (6) or boron (10) or preferably some heavy " reducer " element), and a " neutron converter element " which yields $n(2)$ when bombarded by 60 $n(1)$. An example for such a chain in which carbon acts as reducer and beryllium acts as converter would be the following:

$$C(12) + n(2) = C(13) + n(1)$$
$$Be(9) + n(1) = \text{" } Be(8) \text{ "} + n(2)$$ 65

(" Be(8) " need not mean an existing element, it may break up spontaneously).

One can very much increase the efficiency of the hitherto mentioned 70 neutron chain reactions by having a " neutron multiplicator " O mixed with the elements which take part in the chain reaction. A neutron multiplicator is an element which either splits up $n(2)$ into 75 $n(1) + n(1)$ or an element which yields additional neutrons for instance $n(1)$ when bombarded by $n(1)$. A multiplicator need not be a meta-stable element. Beryllium may be a suitable multipli-80 cator

$$Be(9) + n(1) = \text{" } Be(8) \text{ "} + n(1) + n(1)$$

An efficient particle disappears (and a

PATENT SPECIFICATION

Application Date: March 12, 1934.   No. 7840/34.
"   "   July 4, 1934.   No. 33540/35.

440,023

(No. 33540/35 being divided out of Application No. 19721/34.)

Application Date: Sept. 20, 1934.   No. 27050/34.

One Complete Specification Left: April 9, 1935.

(Under Section 16 of the Patents and Designs Acts, 1907 to 1932.)

Specification Accepted: Dec. 12, 1935.

PROVISIONAL SPECIFICATION
No. 7840 A.D. 1934.

Improvements in or relating to the Transmutation of Chemical Elements

I, LEO SZILARD, a citizen of Germany and Hungary, c/o Claremont Haynes & Co., Vernon House, Bloomsbury, Square, London, W.C.1, do hereby declare the nature of this invention to be as follows:—

It has been demonstrated that if atoms or nuclei, e.g. hydrogen atoms (or protons), heavy hydrogen atoms, referred to from now onwards as diplogen, (or diplogen ions, referred to from now onwards as diplons) etc. are shot at chemical elements, a definite fraction of these shooting particles will cause transmutation in many elements. (How large this fraction is will depend on the nature of the element, the nature of the shooting particle, and its velocity.) If one uses the above mentioned particles and shoots them on light or heavy hydrogen lithium (6) or lithium (7) or other elements a certain proportion of the particles lose their energy through ionizing the substance through which they are shot, and only a fraction of the shooting particles will meet a nucleus of the substance before losing so much energy that the shooting particle is unable to cause transmutation in nuclei which it meets. Of these particles which meet a nucleus in their path (while still being in possession of a sufficiently large fraction of their initial energy) again only a further fraction will be able to penetrate the nucleus, (will be able to cause a transmutation); if the shooting particles are positively charged they are repulsed by the positively charged nucleus, and the probability of their penetrating the nucleus is a function of their relative velocity.

This probability rises rapidly with increasing velocity of the shooting particle and eventually reaches unity at a velocity which depends both on the nature of the shooting particle and the nature of the bombarded element.

However, even if this probability is equal to unity one still has to face the fact that a shooting particle has to travel for instance in air a large distance in order to encounter a nuclear collision (which may cause transmutation), but due to the energy loss which it suffers through ionizing the air its range is comparatively small if its initial velocity corresponds to several million volts energy. Only a fraction of the above mentioned shooting particles can therefore produce transmutation if shot into air or other substances or similar characteristics concerning ionization losses and nuclear collisions.

In accordance with the present invention radio-active bodies are generated by bombarding suitable elements with neutrons, which can be produced in various ways.

In accordance with one feature of the present invention nuclear transmutation leading to the liberation of neutrons and of energy may be brought about by heating up a small area filled with suitable elements very suddenly to high temperature by means of an electric discharge.

RADIO ACTIVE SUBSTANCES.

It is possible to produce elements capable of spontaneous transmutation by bombarding certain elements with fast charged nuclei, for instance by bombarding carbon with protons or aluminium, boron and magnesium with helium ions (particles). However, most of the radio active elements produced by the bombardment of these light elements with protons or alpha particles have a short existence (they disintegrate spontaneously in a time shorter than a few hours to half their amount), and it is not possible to use these charged nuclei for the transmutation of the heavier elements with good efficiency as the ionization loss gets too large. It is, however, possible to produce with good efficiency (both from lighter and heavier elements) radio active sub-

[*Price* 1/-]

FIG. 6(b). First page of Leo Szilard's specification for BPN 440023 secret patent cases from between the two world wars. The records show many assignments of patents to the Admiralty, War Office, and Air Ministry, with the intention of keeping the patents secret. They also show continuing official concern that the patent law was unsatisfactory in this particular aspect, and that it was time for a change.

Another committee on secret patents met on 24 March 1934 to discuss what strategy the fighting departments might adopt to begin the process of patent law reform. That nothing could be done with section 30 of the 1907 Act unless the patentee agreed to assign again emerged as the central problem. The committee's report, dated 30 March 1934, complained that 'there is no power under the Act to enforce assignment in a case where secrecy is considered desirable in the public interest' (PRO: AVIA8/40), and continued by pointing out that an inventor 'who is unmoved by appeals to patriotism or wider commercial interest' could only be subjected to the Official Secrets Act or the prospect of being paid 'sufficient consideration'. Up till then, the committee could confirm that they had been able 'in all cases to rely on the efficacy of threats of the possible consequences of publication under the Official Secrets Act' and avoid any suggestion of a bribe. The committee was forced to conclude that no change in the law was 'practicable or desirable'.

The memoranda that circulated around the Air Ministry, as people there read the committee's report, showed a rather high level of objection to its conclusions. One memorandum gave a good argument for dropping secrecy completely, by giving an example of a current problem. This was the fact that the Air Ministry had in hand no fewer than sixteen patent applications covering gun turret designs, all of which were to be kept secret; a further eleven patent applications were also being considered as possible candidates for secret status. These twenty-seven patents covered eight completely different designs for gun turrets on military aircraft, and only one design would in the end be adopted. It would be far better, the memorandum argued, to publish all the ideas, just to add to the confusion of those outside the service, and then keep secret what was actually being adopted in the Royal Air Force (PRO: AVIA8/40).

This common-sense approach to secrecy comes across in another case, early in 1937, which concerned the hydraulic firing mechanisms for the guns in a military aircraft (PRO: AVIA8/47). In reply to a junior minute stating that 'there are technical reasons why secrecy should be maintained', an official further up the administrative pyramid wrote: 'there is no black magic attached to these inventions ... similar schemes could be produced by any engineer with a knowledge of hydraulics.' Another was to write, taking a more political point of view: 'every European country is exploring this field [hydraulic controls and actuators in aircraft] and must know that we are too. The inference surely will be that we have allowed these [designs] to be published because we have something better.'

We see here a new attitude to secrets emerging, which is far more sensible than that found in Chapters 2 and 3, when the first secret patent law of 1859 was being framed. There had been no real change in the law since then, however, and by 1939 the law would have remained unchanged for eighty years. There had been dramatic change in nearly everything else in the United Kingdom and elsewhere in the world during that time, and the rate of change seemed to be increasing. For example, in just the twenty years between the wars, the time covered in this chapter, Stanley Baldwin had rejuvenated the Tory Party in 1922, the Labour Party had replaced the Whigs as the party of opposition, there had been a general strike, a terrible depression, and, abroad, democracy had been abandoned in two major countries in Europe, Italy and Germany. Finally, and perhaps this was the change at home that would be felt the longest, the United Kingdom itself was no longer one of Great Britain and Ireland, but of only Great Britain and Northern Ireland.

But in 1939 any radical change in the patent law would have been postponed: the Second World War was not only going to take precedence, it was going to precipitate such technical change that 'secrets', once the war was over, were to take on an even more serious character.

8

The Second World War

8.1 The Health of the State

Writing of the Great War of 1914–18, Randolph S. Bourne (1886–1918) put forward the slogan 'War is the Health of the State' in one of his essays (Resek (1964), 71). Bourne also remarked upon the enthusiasm with which men with administrative or managerial expertise had volunteered for military service in the war, 'as if the war and they had been waiting for each other' (ibid. 60). In the Second World War we find a very similar situation with men of technical expertise, the 'boffins' as they were called in the United Kingdom, although the origin of this new word has been lost.

Enthusiasm for a technical fix, a quick technical solution, is not, however, the monopoly of men with technical knowledge. A very unusual essay, undated and unsigned, was written by an Admiralty official, probably in the summer of 1940, entitled 'Inventors without Bars' (PRO: ADM1/11768). In this, we read that 'in the first five months of the present war' the Department of Scientific Research at the Admiralty had 'carefully examined' no fewer than 18,000 ideas put forward by members of the public. These ideas had come from all parts of the world, by post, cable, and telephone, and were usually addressed to the First Sea Lord, but some were to the King or the Prime Minister. It so happened that the Admiralty, as the senior service, had put itself in the position of dealing with all communications of this kind.

What is remarkable is the number of communications this anonymous author could vouch for, as well as the range of people involved. We read of how ideas came in from the unemployed and from employers of thousands, from clergymen and criminals, and from stockbrokers (who took the precaution of writing through their solicitors). Money was sometimes mentioned as a factor, but people writing in from abroad often brought up the possibility of British citizenship, or 'permanent asylum' as the anonymous author put it. And he added, in view of some of the crazy suggestions

offered, 'that the choice of that last word [might have been] un-
fortunate'. Nevertheless, the essay concluded, all these ideas had
been sent to the department with 'the best and most patriotic
motives', and some excellent suggestions could be picked out. These
came most often from people who were already in the services, 'of
all ranks and ratings'.

The Department of Scientific Research was deeply involved with
technical work in a number of establishments, as we shall see, and
their involvement with secret patents was to become extensive. The
outbreak of war, however, meant there were now two distinct ways
of making a patent 'secret': either through section 30 of the 1907
Patents and Designs Act or by using the Defence Regulations.

8.2 DORA

In September 1939 it was the turn of George VI to be 'pleased to
make Regulations' by an Order in Council, as we saw George V
doing back in 1914 (Section 6.6). These regulations, again often
referred to by the acronym DORA (Defence of the Realm Acts),
turn up in various forms in the records concerning patents as the
Second World War progressed. We read of the Defence (General)
Regulations 1939, No. 6 of which gave the comptroller of patents
the very flexible power of being able to, 'not withstanding anything in any Act, omit or delay the doing of anything which he
would otherwise be required to do'. The power to prohibit the
publication anywhere of any ideas contained in a patent application is also found in the Defence Regulations. In 1941 all these
powers, and the penalties that could be imposed upon people who
ignored orders made under the regulations, were confirmed by
Regulation No. 3 of the Defence (Patents, Trade Marks, etc.)
Regulations 1941. We shall see, in Chapter 9, that it was the ideas
contained in these Defence Regulations that were taken into the
new patent law framed in 1949.

The extent to which the Defence Regulations were actually used,
during the Second World War, to prohibit the publication of patents can be seen by referring to the reports from the DSIR. No
reports were issued during the war, but in 1949 a report for 1947–
8 was issued, and this gave a review of the work supported by
the DSIR during the period 1938–48 (BPP 1948–9 (7761), xxi. 49).
A total of 250 patent applications were filed over the ten years

1938–48 by the DSIR, and 'the publication of fifty of the inventions covered by these patents was prohibited by the Comptroller of Patents under powers conferred by the Defence (General) Regulations, 1939, and the Defence (Patents, Trade Marks, etc.) Regulations, 1941'. The report also tells us that only 103 of the patents applied for, secret or not, were finally sealed. The others were allowed to lapse or were abandoned.

DSIR support for research work during the war was modest compared to the support that came directly from the fighting departments. This was to be expected because it was development work that needed support if new ideas were to be applied to winning the war. The result was that patent activity in the Admiralty and in the Air Ministry was very high. For example, an Air Ministry list survives giving details of patent applications coming from the Marconi Company between 1940 and 1948. The list shows a total of eighteen patent applications, all in connection with work supported by the government in the field of electronics, and ten of these were kept secret during the war by means of the Defence Regulations. A footnote to the list emphasizes that none of the patents was made a true secret patent by means of section 30 of the Act of 1907 (PRO: AVIA15/2431).

8.3 The Scientific Advisory Committee

The War Cabinet had a Scientific Advisory Committee during the Second World War. From 1942 to 1947, when it was disbanded, the chairman was Sir Henry Dale (1875–1968), president of the Royal Society and an outstanding physiologist. In November 1942 the battle of Stalingrad had brought about a feeling, as far as the Allies were concerned, that the tide might have turned in the war, and the Scientific Advisory Committee turned some attention to the time when hostilities might be brought to an end. One aspect of this that came up in their deliberations was the hope for a rich harvest of industrial property rights from all the investment in weapons research and development. A subcommittee was formed, early in 1943, to prepare a report on patents that should be forthcoming from war work, and their final confidential report was printed on 9 August 1943 (PRO: AVIA15/2406).

The chairman of the subcommittee was the Minister of Education, R. A. Butler (1902–82). He was joined by Sir Edward

Appleton (1892–1965), who was secretary to the DSIR, and a few other men of scientific eminence. Their final report is interesting because it clearly laid the ground upon which the National Research and Development Corporation was to be founded once the war was over. We shall be looking at the new corporation briefly in Chapter 9.

Concerning the valuable industrial property rights that were to be expected after the war, the final report to the War Cabinet was rather vague. The report was circulated in its draft form to all the fighting departments, and the response was rather unsympathetic, certainly as far as the Air Ministry was concerned. Their director of scientific research, D. F. Pye (1886–1960), who was later, as Sir David Pye, to be provost of University College London, wrote a minute about the draft report. It began: 'A time like this, when one's day is very fully occupied with urgent matters, does not seem to me to be a happy one to produce a report of this kind, concerning wide issues with little relevance to the war effort except this: that the present system of patents requires many hundreds of highly trained men to work it' (PRO: AVIA15/2406). The problem was, he continued, that worrying about patent problems was simply diverting people from more essential work. His remarks proved to be very sensible. Early in 1944, the President of the Board of Trade asked Sir William Palmer (1883–1964), secretary at the Ministry of Production, to preside over a committee that would consider what action should be taken to secure the protection of all the inventions that were expected as a result of the war. At their first meeting, on 21 March 1944, at which the Treasury, all the supply ministries, the Board of Trade, the Post Office, the DSIR, and all the fighting departments were represented, the conclusion was reached that of all patents those in the field of electronics were of the greatest value. Sir Stafford Cripps (1889–1952), the Minister of Aircraft Production, was particularly keen on the idea of priority for electronics and, at a very high-level meeting at the Treasury on 3 August 1944, he called for more people to be put on patents work in the electronics field, and also asked that people who understood US patent law be used for this work (PRO: ADM1/17165).

A minute written in January 1945 tells us that a total of eighty-five patent applications in the field of electronics were prepared by the Admiralty during the war, but that 'valid patents of major commercial importance have proved to be far fewer in number than was originally presumed' (PRO: ADM1/17165).

Sir Stafford Cripps had been mistaken in thinking that patents in the field of electronics were going to be of great value, and the Admiralty minute continued to say that the situation outside the electronics field was just the same. The list of patents they had gave 'no support to the idea that these wartime inventions represent an appreciable national asset'. The same had applied after the First Word War, they added, and this was to be expected: the Admiralty was concerned with weapons, not peaceful applications.

There was one wartime development in electronics, however, that was to be of major commercial importance in peacetime. This was radar, the electronic technique of locating and measuring the position of distant targets. Radar was to become the future method of navigation for ships and aircraft everywhere, and would involve an enormous investment in new electronic hardware. A key device in all the new radar systems was the cavity magnetron, an invention that is usually considered to be entirely a British one.

The story of radar in general and the cavity magnetron in particular has been told by a number of authors (Watt (1957); Bowen (1987); Burns (1988); Rolph (1991)). It is told briefly here, concentrating upon the early history of the cavity magnetron and the patents, all kept closely secret, that were applied for in the hope of protecting the intellectual property rights in this important new device.

8.4   Radar

Simple pulsed radar systems work by sending out a short pulse of radio waves, preferably in a well-defined direction, and then receiving an echo back from the distant target. The range of the target is found from the time-delay between sending and receiving, while the direction of the target is simply the direction defined by the antenna system used for transmitting and receiving. Very short pulses and very short wavelengths are called for if this kind of simple radar system is to have good resolution. As radio waves travel at the velocity of light, 300 metres in one-millionth of a second, pulse widths below one microsecond are needed to resolve something like two aircraft flying closely together. Similarly, wavelengths of a few centimetres are needed if the antenna systems,

hopefully with beam widths of one degree or so, are to be made
small enough to fit into an aircraft: the diameter of the antenna
must be a large number of wavelengths. Thus very short pulse
lengths and very short wavelengths are needed for airborne radar.
Radar for sea navigation is not so demanding, the targets being
much bigger and much further away. Greater range, however, calls
for greater transmitter power, and this is the third parameter in
the radar equation. To sum up: in 1939 there was an urgent need
for a high power, very high frequency, source of radio power that
could be pulse-modulated. It was the cavity magnetron that was to
satisfy this need, which it still does, after over fifty years of further
development.

8.5   The Cavity Magnetron

The Physics Department of the University of Birmingham had
been chosen as one of the centres where research into radar problems would be supported by the Admiralty. The head of department at the time was Professor M. L. E. Oliphant (b. 1901), who
played a major role as a scientific adviser to the British government during the war, particularly in the matter of atomic weapons
(Davis (1969), 112–13). Just before the war started, Oliphant
planned a programme for his department to start work on the
generation and detection of centimetric radio waves, with Admiralty support through a number of contracts (Burns (1988), 259–
83). This programme involved J. Sayers (b. 1912), who was given
the problem of developing high-power centimetric sources, and
J. T. Randall (1905–84), who was asked to concentrate on the
problem of detection.

Sayers took the already well-known klystron oscillator as his
starting-point. This is a high-vacuum device in which a pencil-like
electron beam passes through one or more cylindrical resonant
cavities, the beam passing along the cavity axis. Randall, who had
an able assistant in the graduate student H. A. H. Boot (1917–83),
took as his starting-point the simple magnetron device, which had
been put forward as a possible detector of centimetric waves by its
original Japanese inventor, K. Okabe, in an important review paper
he had published in English several years previously (Okabe
(1930)). The simple magnetron was a high-vacuum diode in which
the cylindrical anode, surrounding the cylindrical cathode, was split

into two semicircular halves. A magnetic field, B, had to be provided along the axis of the device. In its simplest application, as an oscillator, a resonant circuit was connected across the two halves of the anode and the device would work at the gyromagnetic frequency, $(e/m)B$, where e and m are the charge and mass of the electron.

As e/m has the value 28GHz/tesla, and magnetic fields around one tesla are easily provided, the magnetron device is a natural one for the generation of centimetric, even millimetric, radio waves, not for the detection. It was thus hardly surprising that Randall and Boot soon abandoned their chief's original plan and turned from the detection problem towards the problem of generation. The difficulty they had with the magnetron, however, was its cylindrical geometry. In the klystron, the electrons travelled along the axis of the device, and this fitted naturally into the geometry of the cylindrical cavity resonator, which was the obvious choice for a resonator at wavelengths of only a few centimetres. The magnetron, in contrast, with its radial electron flow, seemed to fit in with nothing at all. The magnetic field in the magnetron, however, caused the electrons to spiral around the cathode as they moved radially from cathode to anode, and this had caused a number of workers in the field to try out the idea of a cavity magnetron, in which several cavity resonators were deployed around the circumference of the device to form an anode with a segmented kind of structure.

It seems certain that Randall and Boot had seen only one earlier proposal for a cavity magnetron. This had been published as a US patent by Samuel (1936). They had not noticed Russian work (Alekseev and Malyarov (1940)), which had been published well before the Nazi invasion of the USSR, even though this was in a journal that could be found in many UK libraries. They were also unaware of considerable activity in Japan on cavity magnetrons at the time, work which has been reviewed recently by Nakajima (Burns (1988), ch. 18).

Randall and Boot decided to try out the new kind of magnetron in their own laboratory and came up with their own design. This involved a cylindrical magnetron anode with six holes surrounding the central hole that accommodated the cathode of the device. Slots were cut radially so that each of the six holes was open to the central hole. The form of the device may be seen from the drawing, taken from the patent specification that the Birmingham workers eventually published in 1947, reproduced in Fig. 7. This later version of the cavity magnetron had eight holes in its anode block, instead of the original six, for reasons that will be given below. Randall and Boot coupled their device to the outside world by means of an inductive loop and a coaxial lead. These may be seen, in the eight-hole version, at the top of the figure. The device was tested and the first results were extremely encouraging: high power output was obtained close to the expected frequency.

In a very informative paper that Boot and Randall (1976) published more than thirty years after all these exciting events, they made it clear there was a considerable amount of luck connected with their success. The cavity magnetron worked in a far more complicated way than simple theory might suggest.

8.6   E. C. S. Megaw

The Birmingham workers were also lucky in having the Wembley laboratories of the British General Electric Company take Randall and Boot's first design for a cavity magnetron as the starting-point for a production version of the device. This was desperately needed for radar work, and the team concerned with the development was led by E. C. S. Megaw (1908–56), who had had much experience with magnetrons of the conventional split-anode variety.

In a paper he published after the war Megaw (1946) explained that Randall and Boot's first design, which had six segments in its anode block, was abandoned after the first twelve devices had been made and tested at Wembley. The device was then redesigned to have eight segments, as shown in Fig. 7. The eight-segment version worked far better, and suggests that Megaw and his team may have been more knowledgeable in magnetron theory at the time than might have been expected, or, more probably, that they were guided by their intuition and experience of magnetrons in general. Megaw's team did not just redesign the anode block of the cavity magnetron that originally came from Birmingham. They took two further important steps in its development as a vital device for wartime radar. These were the pulse modulation needed to obtain the very high peak power output that the device was capable of, and, at the same time, the use of an oxide-coated cathode to provide the very high peak emission current that pulse modulation to high power output demanded (Megaw (1946)).

588,185 COMPLETE SPECIFICATION

SHEET .1

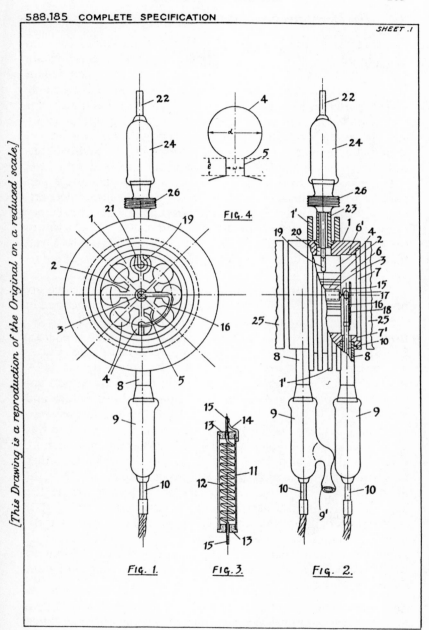

FIG. 7. Drawings in specification, BPN 588185, published May 1947, showing construction of cavity magnetron manufactured at GEC Wembley laboratories in 1941 (Crown Copyright 1947)

8.7 The Magnetron Secret Patents

The director of scientific research (DSR) at the Admiralty, who had placed the contracts supporting the work at Birmingham University, was C. S. Wright, who had looked after Leo Szilard back in 1936 (Section 7.6). Wright was a scientist of remarkably wide experience, having worked at the Cavendish Laboratory for two years before joining the British Antarctic Expedition (1910–13). He served in the Royal Engineers during the Great War, and then had a number of jobs in various Admiralty research laboratories before becoming DSR in 1934, a position he held until 1946.

Patents covering the magnetron work at Birmingham were prepared, early in 1940, at Wright's request, by the Contracts Department at the Admiralty. 'It is thought most unlikely that the secrecy of this invention can be maintained after the War', Wright was to tell Contracts (PRO: ADM1/13811), and for this reason he asked that the Defence Regulations be used to prohibit publication during the war.

The problem of maintaining secrecy in the USA then came up, because, by 1941, the cavity magnetron was to be manufactured in the USA, Canada, and Australia (PRO: ADM1/13922). A letter from Admiralty Contracts, dated 8 August 1941 (PRO: ADM1/13878), to patent agents in Washington, DC, tells us: 'the Admiralty desire that a secrecy order should be issued by the USA Authorities in respect of the USA Application.' This request anticipated the patents agreement to be signed by Lord Halifax and Roosevelt's Secretary of State, Cordell-Hall, that would come into effect on 1 January 1942. The secrecy clause in this agreement was a collector's item of diplomatic elegance: 'When the information, invention, design or process is of a category for which the other Government request secrecy on security grounds, each Government will take such steps as it deems practicable to ensure the appropriate degree of secrecy in manufacture and use' (PRO: ADM1/13899). Problems with secrecy when exchanges of technical information were made between the United Kingdom and its Allies had come up before in the previous world war. Writing to the Treasury solicitor in June 1918, the comptroller of the Patent Office explained:

The United States do not allow what we call Secret Patents but I have made arrangements with their Patent Office for preventing the publication of all inventions which it is considered ought not to be made public. I am afraid that it will be impossible to preserve indefinitely the Secrecy of Secret Patents (proper) in this country if the Invention is communicated to the Allies, but on the other hand, there seems a general opinion that it would not be possible to withhold any inventions which have real importance for the war from our Allies (PRO: BT209/167).

Real importance was certainly the category that the cavity magnetron came into. It was essential to get the device manufactured in large numbers, and this could best be done in the USA. Things were made easier by Wright's decision at the very beginning not to make the patents covering the Birmingham work 'Secret Patents (proper)', as Franks had described them in his letter, but simply to use the Defence Regulations to prohibit publication only during the war. This could then be matched by the Allies issuing similar prohibition orders.

8.8 Problems with the Magnetron Patents

Several patent specifications covering the work on cavity magnetrons at Birmingham University were published in 1947, when the orders prohibiting publication were lifted, but of these only three will be considered here. These are BPN 588185, 588916, and 590546.

BPN 588185 was the first patent that Randall, Boot, and Wright applied for, in August 1940. Entitled 'Improvements in High Frequency Electrical Oscillators', it was accepted on 16 May 1947. The published complete specification describes the eight-segment cavity magnetron with an indirectly heated oxide-coated cathode, the device shown in Fig. 7, which Megaw's team designed. The device described in the provisional specification had only six segments and a simple tungsten filament (PRO: ADM1/13811). BPN 588916 has the same title as 588185, and was applied for by Sayers and Wright on 3 October 1941. The patent was accepted on 6 June 1947, and the printed specification describes the very important idea of adding 'straps' to the magnetron anode block. These straps limit the number of modes of oscillation to the modes that should provide high efficiency and stable operation. Sayers had worked out this idea in the Birmingham laboratories by making careful measurements on magnetron anode blocks, to which he added the strapping connections, and noting the connections that eliminated the unwanted modes. BPN 590546, which also had the same as

588185, was applied for by Boot, Randall, and Wright in February 1942, and accepted in July 1947. The printed specification describes the cavity magnetron with Sayers' straps, but includes some attempt to put a little theory behind the whole thing.

There seems to have been some problems with BPN 588185, and the attempt to solve these problems appears to have been left to Boot. He was the only member of Oliphant's original team to stay on at Birmingham throughout the war. In 1943 Sayers was to join the Manhattan Project, and Randall was to take a temporary lectureship at Cambridge University. As Wright wrote to Sir Edward Appleton, in January 1944: 'When this Group was in full strength under Oliphant, there were altogether twenty three salaried staff employed on [radar electronic device] work.' Now, Wright continued, only six remained, headed by Boot, with three people, all working on the 10 centimetre magnetron, while the other two were working on the 3 centimetre magnetron and other devices (PRO: ADM1/15228). Wright was worried that Birmingham might lose more people. He knew that there were still many problems with the magnetron that called for a solution.

The first sign that BPN 588185 was running into difficulties came in June 1946 when the comptroller at the Patent Office turned down a personal appeal from Wright to allow amendments to be made to the application. An appeal on this was made to Mr Justice Evershed on 4 December 1946, who upheld the comptroller's decision because the amendments proposed would have widened the claims (PRO: ADM1/15188).

In March 1949 Boot took an unusual amount of space in the *Journal* to apply 'under Section 21 of the Acts' to amend the specification of BPN 588185, which had now been printed, and he gave as his reason: 'To render the Specification and Claims self-consistent and to limit the scope of the claims' (*OJ (P)* 3137 at 423–4). This was allowed, and as a result BPN 588185 is an interesting specification to consult. It is in two editions, the second being dated 10 September 1949, more than two years after the first, and the number of claims has been reduced from twenty-nine to only twenty-five.

8.9   Awards to Inventors

The end of the story may be taken from the record of a two-day hearing in May 1949, before the Royal Commission on Awards to Inventors. Randall, Boot, and Sayers were awarded a total of £36,000 for the work they did at Birmingham on the cavity magnetron, and the commissioners made it clear that the question of any income they might or might not have received from their patents was not a factor in the award. The point was that the work had been of outstanding importance to the United Kingdom, and the three inventors had been receiving an income at the time that was considered far too small. This certainly seems to be true for Boot who, the commissioners learnt, received between £150 and £200 per annum at the time.

Randall, in his evidence before the commissioners, was to give an important clue as to what may have gone wrong, or perhaps right, with the cavity magnetron patents from Birmingham. He said:

neither Boot nor myself had any contact with work of this kind before. We came entirely newly into the field and perhaps if I may say so myself, it was all the better for that: that we had no real knowledge of the prior art in the subject at all. We were brought, like many other physicists, into an entirely new field and therefore thought of these things *de novo* (PRO: T166/10).

Here Randall is putting forward a philosophy that is widely held by scientists. To write valuable patents, however, one should not, perhaps, think '*de novo*'. The point is to make clear just where the 'prior art' has taken the problem, and then describe clearly what one's invention has contributed to its solution. This means that there may be many important technical developments that cannot be covered generally in the format of a valuable patent, whereas some details can be. The cavity magnetron may well be an example.

The patents from Birmingham were still being subjected to court hearings in the USA as late as 1956 (PRO: ADM1/22052). Perhaps the most surprising factor in the matter was the propaganda that was put forward in the USA to show that work in the Soviet Union was the true primary source of the idea for the cavity magnetron. The paper by Alekseev and Malyarov (1940) referred to in Section 8.5 was translated and republished in the *Proceedings of the Institute of Radio Engineers* (New York) in March 1944, with an editorial comment that it was now institute policy to translate important foreign work and thus bring it to the attention of readers of the *Proceedings*. If this was indeed the new IRE policy, such policy was at once abandoned.

A second attempt to call attention to the Soviet work was made in 1948 when the definitive text *Microwave Magnetrons* was published. An isometric drawing was specially made for the book (Collins (1948), 7) to show how like a 1948 cavity magnetron the Soviet magnetron of the late 1930s had been.

8.10 The Dambusters

This chapter concludes with a brief look at another invention of the Second World War that involved a secret patent. This is the bouncing bomb, an idea attributed to Sir Barnes Wallis (1887–1979) that has inspired works in film, music, and stained glass. A large number of these bombs were used to breach the Möhne and Eder dams in Germany in a raid by the RAF that took place on 17 May 1943. The raid has been described as 'a most brilliant victory' (Webster and Frankland (1961), 172–8), but it is difficult to see why. The British lost fifty-three airmen and eight of the nineteen aircraft sent out on the raid (Cooper (1982), 77). Over 1,000 civilians were drowned, the vast majority of them Russian and Polish prisoners who had been locked up for the night. Later in their book (1961, pp. 289–92), Webster and Frankland show that 'the raid on the dams did no great damage to German armament production', and that the main effect was the psychological shock to the German public.

The first connection between Wallis and 'the great Möhne Dam', as he called it, may be found in a report he wrote early in 1941 (PRO: ADM1/11767). According to the report, his method of destroying the dam was to 'produce a local earthquake' by exploding a very large bomb, typically 10 tons of high explosive, at a considerable depth in either the water or earth close by the dam. This could be done, Wallis argued, by dropping the bomb from a height of 40,000 feet. He went on to give some calculations on the shock wave that might be produced by such an explosion and to show what effect the shock wave might have when it struck the dam. The report was circulated around the fighting departments and did not meet with much enthusiasm. The problem of dropping bombs from such a great height with any accuracy, particularly under real war conditions, was raised. C. S. Wright commented on the value of the calculation Wallis had made and was clearly not impressed. He ended his minute, dated 6 June 1941: 'Mr Wallace [*sic*] seems to have access to a good deal of confidential information and it would have been better if he had acknowledged his sources' (PRO: ADM1/11767).

Despite the bad start, Wallis lost none of his determination to destroy the Möhne dam. He came up with a very clever solution to the problem of accuracy that must plague any attempt to drop a bomb on a target from an aircraft flying under real war conditions. His solution was to devise a bomb that could be dropped anywhere on the surface of the lake on the high side of the dam, which would then travel over the surface of the water, by bouncing, until it reached the dam wall. The bomb would then promptly sink to the base of the dam wall, where it would explode through the action of a depth-sensing detonator. With such accurate placing, at the very base of the dam wall, the size of the bomb, Wallis argued, could now be much smaller. Wallis worked out all the details of his bouncing bomb during June 1942, while at his employers', Vickers Armstrong at Weybridge (PRO: AVIA15/3933). A patent application, No. 11252/42, was filed at the Patent Office on 11 August 1942, and a copy was sent 'for confidential information only' to the Ministry of Aircraft Production, which informed the Admiralty on 27 August (PRO: ADM1/11767). By 7 September a prohibition order had been issued under the Defence Regulations, making the patent secret. The rest of the story is well known. The bouncing bomb was developed into an operational weapon in well under a year.

The patent became BPN 937959, and the first page of the specification is shown in Fig. 8. This shows that it was not published until 25 September 1963, more than twenty years after its application date. This is a record delay, and there is no explanation given anywhere on the specification. Another interesting feature about this patent is that, although it was applied for in 1942, it has been filed under the Patents Act of 1949 (which has yet to be considered here, and will be the main subject of Chapter 9). That is why the name of the inventor has been displayed prominently in the heading of the specification. The application was made, in this case, by another party.

There was an unexpected sequel to the story of the dambuster bomb as a result of the interrogation of Rheinhold Lambrich in Berlin on 28 May 1945. Lambrich led a group that had developed a spherical bouncing bomb in Germany during the war. Their final

937,959

PATENT SPECIFICATION

DRAWINGS ATTACHED

Inventor: BARNES NEVILLE WALLIS

937,959

Date of filing Complete Specification (under Section 3`(3) of the Patents Act, 1949): Aug. 11, 1942.

Application Date: Aug. 11, 1942.   No. 11252/42.

Application Date: July 9, 1943.   No. 11197/43.

Complete Specification Published: Sept. 25, 1963.

© *Crown Copyright 1963.*

Index at acceptance:—Classes 9(1), A2(B4:B9:E:H:X14), A5(C5B:CX5:D); and 9(2), G3.
International Classification:—F07f. (F07j).

COMPLETE SPECIFICATION

Improvements in Explosive Missiles and means for their Discharge

We, VICKERS AIRCRAFT HOLDINGS LIMITED, formerly Vickers - Armstrongs (Aircraft) Limited, a Company organised under the Laws of Great Britain, of Vickers
5 House, Broadway, Westminster, London, S.W.1, do hereby declare the nature of this invention, and in what manner the same is to be performed, to be particularly described and ascertained in and by the following state-
10 ment:—

Torpedoes as at present used for attacking naval vessels and shipping are disadvantageous on account of the comparative ease with which a target vessel can manoeuvre to avoid
15 a hit, the low speed of the torpedo travelling under its own power coupled with the conspicuous wake or trail of bubbles frequently affording a navigator ample warning to enable him to steer his craft out of danger, whether
20 the torpedo be discharged from an air- or water-borne vessel.

The present invention provides means for executing a novel method of attack, comprising means for supporting an explosive
25 missile and imparting thereto a spinning motion about a horizontal axis at right angles to the direction of attack, release gear for freeing the missile from said supporting means whilst in the spinning condition, and means
30 for positively impelling it towards the target. Where the attack is carried out over a water surface, against shipping or stationary structures, such as hydroelectric dams, locks and like works, the direction of spin imparted to
35 the missile is such that its undersurface rotates towards the target; the effect of such reverse spin is to endue the missile with a certain degree of aerodynamic lift, modifying the effect of acceleration due to gravity
40 so as to decrease the angle of impact with the water surface and thus increase the length of trajectory. Where, on the other hand, the attack is carried out across the land surface,

against targets of relatively small size, such
45 as canals and canal-locks, and other targets which are otherwise unsuitable as ordinary bombing objectives, the effective range is prolonged by imparting a forward spin to the missile, i.e. with its upper surface rotat-
50 ing towards the target; the effect of such forward spin is to enable the missile to override minor obstacles in its path, though it will be evident that this method of attack cannot be adopted where the target is protected
55 by belts of trees, buildings or similar natural or artificial defences.

When the missile is discharged from an aircraft the speed of movement of the aircraft is such that additional means of pro-
60 jection are not required, and in this case the carrier aircraft itself constitutes the projection apparatus inasmuch as it discharges the missile when moving directly towards the target. Alternatively, the missile may be pro-
65 jected from a water-borne carrier moving towards or away from the target at a predetermined speed and height of missile above the water surface, a catapult or other means of projection being provided to discharge the
70 missile while it is in a spinning condition. Where necessary, such catapult or the like may be arranged for broadside discharge.

A missile in accordance with the invention comprises a casing enclosing an explosive
75 charge and a detonator, and means whereby the missile is adapted for support by a carrier aircraft or vessel so as to be capable of co-operating with mechanism thereon for spinning the missile about a horizontal axis at
80 right angles to the intended direction of projection. The detonator may be of a kind which is operated hydrostatically in cases where it is intended that the missile shall not explode until it has reached a certain depth after
85 striking a target.

The missile is preferably of spherical,

[*Price 4s. 6d.*]

FIG. 8. First page of specification, BPN 937959, Sir Barnes Wallis's bouncing bomb (Crown Copyright 1963)

design contained 300 kilograms of high explosive and could bounce along on the water for 1.5 kilometres. It had never been used in service, but was ready at the end of the war and intended for use against shipping (PRO: ADM1/17278). Wallis received the report of the interrogation in November 1945, and wrote back to the Ministry of Aircraft Production with some highly critical remarks about the German theoretical work, which had been translated for him to read. He thought it was 'sententious to a degree, and goes back to Newton on all possible occasions', but the work in England 'carried the analysis of the whole phenomenon' of bouncing over water much further. The surprise, however, is that Wallis wrote that the German workers had ignored the importance of surface tension. Why he made such a criticism is difficult to understand. Surface tension cannot possibly play any significant part in the dynamics of such a turbulent and violent process as takes place when a bomb, or anything else, bounces over the surface of the water.

Webster and Frankland (1961, p. 301) pay tribute to 'the special Wallis weapons' in their official history of the strategic air offensive against Germany, as a factor in Bomber Command's success. These weapons were not only the well-known bouncing bomb. After the breaching of the Möhne and Eder dams in 1943, Wallis's work was looked upon more sympathetically by the authorities, and his 12,000 pound Tallboy bomb was developed. Bombs of this kind were used to destroy the 45,000 ton German battleship *Tirpitz* on 12 November 1944 (ibid. 191).

8.11 Conclusions

This chapter on the Second World War has made no mention of two great secrets kept at the time: the British secret of Bletchley Park and the secret work in the United States on the atomic bomb. The atomic bomb will feature prominently in Chapter 9, because it had an important influence upon the development of patent law from the point of view of secrecy. Bletchley Park, in contrast, concealed an activity that continues today as secretly as ever. For completeness, an outline of the case must be given.

The effective encoding and decoding of secret dispatches in peacetime has been a problem for all governments for centuries. In wartime its solution becomes essential. The article on cryptography in the *Encyclopaedia Britannica* (*EB*11, 7 at 565–6) tells us about the encoding and decoding activities of the Spartan military command some 2,500 years ago and, rightly, emphasizes the major role played by Englishmen, from Francis Bacon (1561–1626) onwards, in publishing their ideas on the development of the art. During the Second World War the British government's codebreaking activities were concentrated at Bletchley Park. By the end of the war no fewer than 4,000 people were working at Bletchley, and yet it was never bombed by the Germans and its remarkable success in decoding almost all enemy military communications went undetected.

Many facts about the work at Bletchley are given in the first volume of the official history of British intelligence during the Second World War (Hinsley (1979)) and also in the later volumes (ii to v) where the topic is found indexed under 'Government Code and Cypher School', the official name for the establishment at Bletchley Park. A considerable amount of new material has been published recently (Hinsley and Stripp (1993)), which includes a number of photographs of the hardware involved. A biography of the mathematician Alan Turing (Hodges (1983)), one of the most remarkable people who worked at Bletchley during the war, gives further impressions of the work there. No British secret patents have been found in the records that might involve the work at Bletchley Park. The extraordinary feature is that Bletchley's achievements either went undetected by the enemy or were simply not thought credible.

9

Making Wartime Procedure Permanent

9.1   The Atomic Bomb

The war with Japan ended in August 1945, a few days after atomic bombs had been dropped on the cities of Hiroshima and Nagasaki. The unexpectedness of this latter event was without precedent. The explosions were over 2,000 times the intensity of any previous explosion caused by a bomb dropped from an aircraft.

The secrecy associated with the development of this new weapon may have been the cause of the public surprise when it came to be used in the war. This secrecy has not been satisfactorily analysed, and the case is a difficult one. That there was such a thing as 'atomic energy' had been well known for many years: the thirteenth edition of the *Encyclopaedia Britannica*, published in 1926, had an article entitled 'Atomic Energy', written by F. W. Aston, Nobel prizewinner and author of the seminal text *Isotopes*. Aston's article explained that the sun's energy came from the fusion reaction of hydrogen into helium, and that it might be possible for mankind to use this source of energy in the distant future, but he was not very optimistic on this point. The possibility of releasing atomic energy by means of fission of the heavy elements was not, of course, mentioned in the article because the discovery of uranium fission by Otto Hahn and Fritz Strassmann was not published until January 1939. Jungk, however, has pointed out that Ida Noddack suggested the possibility of fission as early as 1934 (Jungk (1958), 69). It should also be noted that the secret patent Leo Szilard wrote in 1934 (see Section 7.6) mentioned the possibility of a chain reaction in uranium, but said nothing about fission.

The release of atomic energy was not then, in the 1940s, an idea that was unfamiliar, but it was something most people would have expected to lie far in the future. It was the kind of development put forward in the science fiction of the time. When this atomic energy literally burst upon the scene in August 1945, the surprise was more a case of suddenly finding oneself in the future than of being kept out of a secret. The speed of the new development was the surprise, for it meant that a very large number of people must have been employed as workers on the project. The facts, when they were disclosed, showed that this had indeed been the case.

That the enormous Manhattan Project had been going on, apparently in absolute secrecy, may have been why many people believed that there really was a 'secret', in the old-fashioned sense of the word, about the atomic bomb: one had to know the magic words. Certainly, as Davis suggests, President Truman thought along such lines. He reports the conversation between Truman and Robert Oppenheimer (Davis (1969), 260), and tells how Truman believed that the Russians would never be able to build the bomb because they would never learn the secret. This primitive faith in secrets is in great contrast to the sophisticated attitude we saw at the end of Chapter 7, when the British Air Ministry officials, of the late 1930s, were suggesting that openness was the best policy because it was know-how that mattered, not some 'secret' that could be written down on a piece of paper. In the late 1940s, in contrast, 'secrets' were thought to be what mattered, and this is shown by the legislation that came to be applied to atomic energy on both sides of the Atlantic.

9.2   The McMahon Act of 1946

In November 1945 a United Nations commission was set up to attempt the framing of some kind of control for the future use of atomic energy (Pringle and Spigelman (1982), 47–55). At the time there was hope that the future manufacture of all atomic weapons could be completely banned by the international ownership, control, and inspection of all sources of fissionable material and all nuclear laboratories and installations. These hopes came to nothing. By June 1946 negotiations between the superpowers had broken down and the United States began test atomic explosions at Bikini Atoll.

Attempts in the US Congress to bring in legislation to control the future of atomic weapons, and atomic energy, in the USA itself were made during the winter of 1945–6. The final outcome was the McMahon Act, which became law in August 1946. This set up the Atomic Energy Commission (AEC), and appeared to give civilian control of all atomic matters. As Davis (1969, p. 263) has pointed out, however, in an emergency all control passed to the Pentagon. The point about the McMahon Act, for the purpose of this book, is that it completely prohibited any exchange of information with other nations on atomic energy matters: not only information on atomic weapons, but *all* aspects of atomic energy were now to be kept secret.

9.3 The Atomic Energy Act of 1946

In the United Kingdom a bill to control atomic energy had been introduced in the House of Commons early in 1946 and published on 1 May (BPP 1945–6 (113), i. 157). The bill is of great interest here because it proposed strict control, and imposed unprecedented powers of secrecy, not only upon patent specifications but also upon the simplest kinds of information exchange between workers who, by any stretch of the imagination, could be considered workers in the field of atomic energy.

The bill had two clauses, which came through Parliament virtually unscathed to become sections 11 and 12 of the Atomic Energy Act 1946 (9 & 10 Geo. VI, c. 80). These two sections are worth looking at in some detail. Let us consider section 12 first, the section that dealt with patents. Section 12 required the comptroller of patents to inform the minister of any patent application that appeared to relate 'to the production or use of atomic energy or research into matters connected therewith'. The minister needed only to know that the application existed; no details needed to be given. Once that was done, the comptroller, 'not withstanding anything in any Act', could 'omit or delay the doing of anything which he would otherwise be required to do in relation to the application'. These words are the same as those used in the Defence Regulations, made by Order in Council back in 1939 and 1941. Section 12 continued, again following the precedent laid down by the Defence Regulations, to give the comptroller the power to prohibit publication of the contents of the application anywhere, and also to allow the minister to inspect all the documents. If, as a result of the minister's inspection, it became clear that 'the invention is not of importance for purposes of defence', then everything went back, without prejudice, into the normal mode of procedure laid down by the old patent law of 1907.

Section 11 of the Atomic Energy Act was a far more serious

matter than section 12, because it introduced something quite new. It made it an offence to communicate, without the consent of the minister, in any way any information about 'plant', existing or proposed, that produced or used atomic energy. Section 11 went on to include not only 'plant' but 'purpose or method of operation of' and 'process operated or proposed to be operated in' such plant. Everybody resident in the United Kingdom came under this law, of course, not simply those employed in the atomic energy industry. The Act thus covered a conversation between two students speculating about some idea for a new kind of reactor: if they had not first asked and obtained the minister's permission, they would have been committing an offence. Clearly, this was a wide-ranging piece of legislation and, as would be expected, it became law only after some interesting debate in Parliament.

9.4   An Unusual Debate

Throughout this book, the arrival of a new piece of patent legislation has been used as an opportunity to report briefly on the events in Parliament as the new bill came under discussion. Up to now, it has been noted that Parliament had very little to say about the principles of keeping secrets. If there was any debate on these 'secret' matters, it concerned the compensation that might be due to inventors who got involved with problems of this kind. The debate in 1946 on the Atomic Energy Bill did not follow this old tradition at all. This may have been due to the fact that the British Parliament had fallen out with its old traditions: for the first time in its history a general election, on 26 July 1945, had given a large majority to the Labour Party.

Although the Atomic Energy Bill had been published on 1 May 1946, it did not have its second reading until 8 October. The reason for this delay was probably to allow time to see the outcome of the United States legislation: the McMahon Act (Section 9.2) had become law on 1 August.

The second reading (*PDC* 427 at 43–98, 113–46) was introduced by the Prime Minister, Clement Attlee, who noted the world-wide concern about the problems of atomic energy after the bombing of Hiroshima and Nagasaki, and the hope everywhere for the eventual prohibition of atomic weapons. He indicated clauses 4 and 5 of the bill, which gave very wide powers of entry

and inspection of any premises, public or private, where there was
any reason to believe atomic energy work might be under way,
and he admitted that these clauses-'might appear very drastic. . . .
We are taking steps which any Government must take in dealing
with an invention of such immense potential destruction; and
whether they are private activities or public activities they must
be subject to close governmental supervision.' Turning to clause
11, discussed above as section 11 of the Act, Attlee described it as
merely control of know-how. Clause 12, he went on, gave:

power to control and restrict the publication of information about atomic
energy patent applications, pending notification of the Minister of Supply,
who can inspect documents and decide whether the subject matter is of
military importance. If it is, the prohibition on publication will stand; if
not, the inventor will be free to exploit his invention and the inventor, if
there is a ban, can still offer his invention to the Government.

This final point is important because it reminds us that the patent
law of 1907 was still in place in 1946. Assignment was required
before the secret patent procedure could go ahead.

The opposition made it clear that they would support the Atomic
Energy Bill. The Tory MP for South Kensington, who spoke after
the Prime Minister, said: 'it is going to be impossible to establish
international control unless we first have established national control.' This is a good example of connecting two ideas as though
one followed from the other, when it is very possible that these
two ideas exclude one another. It was also putting a label 'control'
on to a bill that was, by means of the very secrecy clauses being
discussed here, going to make any kind of open, public, or demo-
cratic control of atomic energy impossible.

There had been, early in 1946, a world-wide hope for, and a
belief in the possibility of, a ban on future atomic weapons. By
October, when the second reading was taking place, the public
may still have believed in this possibility but, as Gowing has noted,
the British Air Ministry had already placed the requisition for an
atomic bomb with the Ministry of Supply in August 1946 (Gowing
(1974), i. 467). The secret British bomb programme had already
started. As Pringle and Spigelman (1982, p. 137) remark, even
Winston Churchill, when he returned as Prime Minister in 1951,
was amazed to find how he had been kept unaware of the bomb
programme, its progress and expense.

Against this background, one protest against the secrecy clauses in the Atomic Energy Bill is worth noting. It came from James Ranger (1889–1975), a member of the radical Independent Labour Party in his youth, who had been a Labour candidate for Parliament in many elections before becoming MP for Ilford South in 1945. Ranger could see clearly what the secrecy clauses in the bill implied and, in what was his maiden speech, he went straight for them:

if our secrecy Clauses are intended to cover the operation of illegal manufacture of illegal weapons, it is better that those Clauses should never appear.... Our salvation lies not in building up a national control of this new power, but in putting everything we have, all our time and energies and enthusiasm, into the idea of international control and the outlawing of atomic warfare. I ask for a withdrawal of these Clauses ... as an indication of that determination, and as having a psychological effect which will help the Foreign Secretary in international conferences and in his work in trying to disperse suspicion, now hampering and obstructing work that is essential to our welfare and very existence (*PDC* 427 at 69–72).

Ranger was not the only MP to speak against the secrecy clauses of the bill. On both sides of the House, concern was expressed about their implications. The Minister of Supply, towards the end of the debate, responded by saying that clause 11 was 'the best compromise we have been able to devise' between the contradictions of national security and the freedom needed for the exchange of scientific knowledge. All the objections to clause 11 could be answered, he assured the House, by the fact that he could make orders excluding certain people from the restrictions of clause 11. This certainly happened. Clause 11 became section 11 of the Act, and it stands today as a statute in force. An example of the kind of exclusion the minister mentioned can be found in the Act that set up the United Kingdom Atomic Energy Authority (UKAEA) in 1954. This Act excludes all employees of the UKAEA from section 11 of the Atomic Energy Act of 1946: they have agreed to conditions of employment that cover the problem.

Finally, what did the minister think of James Ranger's maiden speech? He dismissed it as an argument that 'we in this country ... simply [refuse] to go on with the science and production of atomic energy'. Perhaps Ranger was not sorry when, in 1950, he was not re-elected as an MP and was never one again.

9.5 Preparing for a Change

The Atomic Energy Act of 1946 had changed the law only for atomic energy patents. In all other cases, as we noted at the end of Chapter 7, there had been no real change in the secret patent law since the first Act covering the problem was passed in 1859. In April 1944 the Board of Trade had appointed a committee, under the chairmanship of the distinguished barrister K. R. Swan, later Sir Kenneth (1877–1973), to collect evidence and make proposals for changes in the patent law generally. The Swan Committee produced two interim reports (BPP 1944–5 (6618), v. 421; 1945–6 (6789), xiv.'155) and a final report (BPP 1946–7 (7206), xiii. 457). Taken together, these reports give an excellent review of the patent law as it stood at the time, not only in the UK but elsewhere. The final report proposed changes to help with compulsory working, licensing, dealing with monopolies and cartels, restrictive practices, and the reduction of costs for patentees. In the main, however, the Swan Committee was concerned with the details of court procedure and law. No radical changes of any kind were put forward in the area of secret patents: section 30 of the Patents and Designs Act of 1907 was to be left virtually unchanged.

This was not to the liking of officials in the fighting departments who were to send their comments on the Swan Committee's report, and on the draft legislation, directly to the Board of Trade. A large bundle of papers concerning this correspondence (PRO: BT209/379) begins with a three-page memorandum from the Admiralty. Dated 21 June 1948, the Admiralty memorandum declared that section 30 should be completely scrapped. 'Section 30 has for many years been regarded as something of an oddity', it remarked, and went on to quote 'a recent unreported case [where] Mr Justice Varley made the following remarks':

The whole idea of a patent and the very name patent indicates it is something laid open for inspection. If it is turned into a Secret patent it becomes a latent patent, that is to say, a patent which is not laid open for inspection but which is concealed from inspection. . . . This is one of the most extraordinary contradictions in terms you can possibly imagine—a Secret patent.

But the problem was not just one of oddness, the memorandum continued. Section 30 could work only if the patentee assigned his rights to the Crown. In contrast, the Defence Regulations allowed publication to be prohibited, and this could 'be applied to any application [for a patent], irrespective of its ownership or the owner's whims'. The Defence Regulations were still in force, the machinery was all set up and working in the Patent Office, and the Admiralty considered these regulations to be the ideal solution to the problem.

The Patent Office commented on the Admiralty's memorandum, agreeing that prohibition of publication was the best solution. It would then be up to the fighting department concerned to get a copy of the prohibited application in confidence 'from the applicant (they do not have access to our copy *except in atomic energy cases*') (emphasis added). This last comment reminds us that the Atomic Energy Act 1946 was now in operation. We shall see, towards the end of this chapter, that it was not, in fact, always easy to get copies of prohibited applications: there were so many prohibiting authorities in certain cases. An additional complication was that the Admiralty, as their memorandum made clear, fully accepted 'the proposition that pending Patent Applications must be treated within the Patent Office as "Confidential" and cannot be inspected save with the Applicant's consent' (PRO: BT209/379).

A letter from the head of patents at the Ministry of Supply to the Treasury solicitor, dated 16 November 1948, made a concise summary of what he thought should be done about the old section 30 when the new Patents Bill was drafted. He pointed out that the Patent Office made no use of section 30 at that time. They still had powers under the Defence Regulations until the end of 1950, and now they had section 12 of the new Atomic Energy Act. 'These powers of prohibition are vastly preferable to the archaic machinery of Section 30', he wrote. The problem with the old law, he continued, was that the Patent Office had to bargain with the inventor to get assignment (PRO: BT209/379).

Parliamentary Counsel was clearly thinking along similar lines. Writing to Sir Harold Saunders (1885–1965), the comptroller-general of the Patent Office, Counsel enclosed his draft for the new secret patent clauses that might go into the new bill. This was on 18 November 1948, and Counsel explained that his draft was in response to the Admiralty memorandum of 21 June. 'The old Section 30 should be scrapped and replaced by permanent provisions on the lines of Regulations 3(1) and (2) of the Defence

(Patents, Trade Marks, etc.) Regulations 1941', Counsel wrote, and he continued to give some details behind his thoughts on drafting the new clause: 'I understand that what actually happens is not that the Comptroller receives "advice" from the appropriate department before he puts a stop on the proceedings, but that he puts a stop on first and obtains the advice thereafter.... [I would like] to give express statutory recognition to actual practice' (PRO: BT209/526). The new Patents and Designs Bill was ready in February 1949, and was given a first reading in the House of Lords on 8 March 1949.

9.6 The Patents and Designs Bill of 1949

The second reading of the new bill in the Lords was on 29 March 1949. Lord Lucas of Chilworth, in his introduction, summarized the proposed changes in the patent law as follows. First, the 'true and first inventor' would now be allowed to assign his rights and yet need no longer be involved with the administrative tasks of the application, although his name would have to be on the final specification. Secondly, there were some attempts to eliminate the abuse of the old law to obtain unfair monopolies. Thirdly, Crown use was tidied up. And, finally, there was a need for change in the procedure for securing secrecy. The old procedure, Lord Lucas explained, 'is cumbrous and can be resorted to only when the patent has been assigned, and the provisions have proved to be insufficient in recent years'. The new bill, he said, 'makes permanent the war-time procedure' (*PDL* 161 at 759).

The bill went through the Lords with little change, and no change at all in the secrecy clause, to be introduced to the House of Commons by the President of the Board of Trade, Harold Wilson, on 29 June 1949 (*PDC* 466 at 1408). The second reading and committee stages all went smoothly, and the bill received royal assent on 30 July 1949. The important Acts, however, were the consolidating Acts that came into the legislative process that summer, and received royal assent on the same day. These are the Patents Act 1949 (12, 13 & 14 Geo. VI, c. 87) and the Designs Act 1949 (12, 13 & 14 Geo. VI, c. 88).

The section covering secret patents in the Patents Act of 1949 is section 18. This completely changed the old procedure, by that time virtually unchanged for ninety years, of 'sealing up' and 'keeping secret'. The new law was most detailed in laying down the procedure for prohibiting the publication of the patent application. It was no longer the document itself that was the object of secrecy but its content. The comptroller of patents was given the power of 'prohibiting or restricting the publication of information with respect to the invention, or the communication of such information to any person or class of persons specified'. The comptroller did this only when the patent application appeared to describe an invention that was 'one of a class notified to him by a competent authority as relevant for defence purposes'. If a prohibition order was issued by the comptroller, then subsections 2(*a*) and 2(*c*) of section 18 required him to reconsider the situation after nine months, or at any earlier time, and if publication was no longer 'prejudicial to the defence of the realm', then all could go ahead as usual. If prohibition had to be maintained, then the situation had to be reconsidered at least once a year.

What had happened to the old tradition of confidentiality that the Patent Office, as we saw in Chapter 6, so bravely defended under the direction of Sir Cornelius Dalton, and had continued to defend ever since? The Act of 1949 made no changes to this tradition because, although the inventor was now prohibited from even talking about his invention to anyone, the Patent Office could continue to examine his patent application and take it forward to the stage where it would be accepted. Once that stage was reached, the fighting departments, now termed the 'competent authorities', could see the full text of the specification without any permission being required from the inventor. He was now, of course, fully protected by his patent, even if he could not, in fact, do anything with it. Naturally, most inventors would be happy to co-operate right from the start, so there would be no problems with the procedure. As we have seen, many inventors would even be anxious to precipitate the secrecy process in order to call attention to the importance of their ideas. There may, however, have been the odd case where things did not go smoothly, because there is a letter from the comptroller to the Ministry of Supply on this problem, written towards the end of September 1949, when the new Acts had all been passed but were not to come into effect until the new year. The comptroller made the new situation clear:

Under the new Act the Comptroller maintains prohibition on the advice of a competent authority which includes your Department . . . and the effect of the prohibition . . . is to provide for inspection of the specification by the competent authority on its acceptance . . . whilst bringing in the compensation provisions . . . If therefore, when the new Act comes into force [on 1 January 1950], a prohibition thereunder is applied to cases such as these, they could proceed to acceptance and then would be available for your inspection (PRO: BT209/380).

But, the comptroller is saying, just as his predecessors had to, you are not seeing them now! The Patent Office kept to its old traditions.

This chapter concludes with an account of one case in which the new secret patent procedure was used and the documents describing what happened have been recently made public.

9.7 The Case of the Hovercraft

In a recent book on hovercraft technology, the editor, in his preface, writes: 'The hovercraft is rarely able to compete economically with conventional modes of transportation in their traditional environments. But its amphibious versatility, marine speed and low footprint pressure have given it a role in specialized applications' (Amyot (1989), p. v). This is an accurate summary of the situation in the 1990s, as a glance at the most recent edition of *Jane's High-Speed Marine Craft* (Trillo (1992–3)) will confirm. Hovercraft are manufactured today by a number of firms world-wide. They find many applications with the military, and in commerce their amphibious versatility means that the simplest docking facilities are all that are needed to set up a fast and, provided the sea is fairly calm, comfortable ferry service for both passengers and cars.

There is, in fact, an air-cushion vehicle industry today and, as Hogg has written, 'This whole industry owes its inception to one man: Sir Christopher Cockerell' (Hogg (1970), 17–18). We are concerned here with the very early patents that Cockerell filed on his hovercraft ideas. These patents were filed in 1955 and 1957, but it did not become widely known that there had been some problems with secrecy attached to them until the Earl of Halsbury told the House of Lords about it in 1977 (*PDL* 379 at 270–1). More details of the case were made public in 1991 (PRO: ADM1/26508; AVIA65/1517, 1804).

9.8   *The Early Hovercraft Patents*

C. S. Cockerell was born in 1910, graduated in engineering from
Cambridge University and worked for fifteen years in electronics
with the Marconi Company. In 1950 he set up on his own with a
family business, Ripplecraft, at Somerlyton near Lowestoft, on the
inland waterways of East Anglia known as the Broads. Ripplecraft
were boat-builders, and also offered storage and mooring facilities.
According to a chronology Cockerell submitted to the English
Electric Company in March 1958, he began work with models,
which eventually led him to the hovercraft idea, as early as 1953
(PRO: AVIA65/1804). His first patent application, which led to
BPN 854211, was filed on 12 December 1955, and he tried to
interest a number of firms in his hovercraft idea during 1955 and
in early 1956, without success.

On 29 October 1956 the world was faced with a crisis that may
have had some influence on what happened next in the hovercraft
story. The crisis was brought about by the invasion of Egypt by
Israel, which, in turn, caused the United Kingdom and France to
launch an offensive against military targets in Egypt. Normal use
of the Suez Canal was impossible in the circumstances and, in any
case, by 16 November, the canal was blocked by the scuttling of
forty-nine ships.

It was against this dramatic background that Cockerell asked a
well-connected neighbour of his, Lord Somerlyton (1889–1959),
to communicate details of his invention to the First Sea Lord,
who, at the time, was Lord Mountbatten (1900–79). Lord
Somerlyton wrote to Lord Mountbatten on 8 November 1956, and
on 12 November the Department of Research Programmes and
Planning (DRPP) at the Admiralty, which had replaced C. S.
Wright's old department as the one that dealt with inventions,
received a note from Lord Mountbatten: 'I should be grateful if
you would let me know if there is anything in this invention and
whether it would be worth while to arrange a trial for the Navy'
(PRO: ADM1/26508). A copy of the patent application, which
Cockerell had sent through Lord Somerlyton, and other details,
photographs of models, and so on, were enclosed.

A demonstration of Cockerell's model hovercraft was duly arranged, and took place on 16 November at the offices of his patent
agent, Haseltine, Lake and Company, at 28 Southampton Buildings,

just a few steps away from the Patent Office. Present at the demonstration were the inventor, his brother, his patent agent, two senior technical officers from the Ministry of Supply (MoS), and two more from the Royal Naval Scientific Service (RNSS). The secretary of DRPP reported back to Lord Mountbatten on 20 November: 'the invention ... has been demonstrated to senior technical officers of the Admiralty and the Ministry of Supply and is being investigated in secrecy with Mr. Cockerell's cooperation'. The file (PRO: ADM1/26508) also tells us about the demonstration. The model was about 18 inches in diameter, weighed about 5 pounds and was powered by a 5 cubic centimetre internal combustion engine of the kind used by model aircraft constructors. It flew about 1.5 inches above the floor, at about 10 miles per hour, and was damaged during the demonstration.

A minute by N. D. Imrie, head of patents at DRPP, dated 19 November 1956, tells us what was decided about Cockerell's patent application:

The invention is the subject of pending British Patent Application No. 35656/55 filed 12th. December, 1955, and not so far prohibited by the Patent Office. The inventor was ready to file corresponding Patent Applications abroad and wished to do so in USA, Canada, France, Western Germany and Italy, but not if the invention might be of military value to Her Majesty's Government.

It was also agreed that for a few months the invention shall be classified as SECRET and the Patent Office invited, both by Ministry of Supply and Admiralty, to issue a Prohibition Order on the relevant Patent Application (PRO: ADM1/26508).

Here we see the new secret patent procedure under the 1949 Act in operation. The same day, 19 November, saw the correct form, SY25, leaving the Admiralty for the Patent Office, marked for the attention there of Mr W. Glass, asking him to 'issue a Prohibition Order on Admiralty account under Section 18 of the Patents Act, 1949, in respect of British Patent Application No. 35656/55 under Heading no. 11 and 16 of the Admiralty Stop List' (PRO: ADM1/ 26508).

We can only guess, of course, that the 'Admiralty Stop List', clearly a list already lodged at the Patent Office, was the list of key words that an examiner at the Patent Office had to bear in mind when checking if a patent application might be 'one of a class notified to him by a competent authority as relevant for defence purposes', as section 18(1) of the Act (12, 13 & 14 Geo. VI, c. 87) puts it.

Cockerell's first hovercraft patent, BPN 854211, was kept secret for more than 'a few months' because it was not published until 16 November 1960, just under four years after the request for prohibition. The reasons for this long delay were complex. The potential of the hovercraft in anti-submarine warfare was discussed (PRO: AVIA65/1517) and this may have been a factor in maintaining secrecy. All the calls for secrecy, however, came from the Ministry of Supply, who wanted secrecy maintained while further experimental work could be done. The MoS wanted to keep costs down as well, and this slowed things up. A development contract was finally set up in May 1957 with Saunders Roe. This was initially worth £6,725, and was for further model tests. The contract was extended, for a further £775, to May 1958 (PRO: AVIA65/1804).

The Admiralty, in contrast, seemed to lose interest in the hovercraft, and hovercraft secrets, fairly rapidly. This is shown by the fact that the Admiralty file (PRO: ADM1/26508) contains a leaflet from a department store, the Army and Navy Stores, only a short walk from the old Admiralty offices at Queen Anne's Gate, advertising the new Hoover Constellation vacuum cleaner. This floating vacuum cleaner, one of the RNSS officers had minuted, perhaps unkindly, bore some resemblance to Cockerell's hovercraft. The Hoover Constellation was undoubtedly a very popular innovation of the 1950s. It was first patented in the USA in 1954, and is the subject of BPN 767647, which was filed on 18 March 1955, more than nine months before Cockerell's first hovercraft application. The idea of air-cushion vehicles and air cushions of all kinds was, indeed, in the air.

Cockerell filed two more patent applications in May 1957, and these were promptly made secret by the Ministry of Supply, not to be published until 1962 when they appeared as BPN 893715 and 895341. Both cover developments of the hovercraft idea, and, as with the first patent, BPN 854211, there is no explanation on the printed specification for the delay in publication.

9.9   The National Research and Development Corporation

By early March 1958, it became clear to Cockerell that the MoS were not going to renew the hovercraft development contract with

Saunders Roe. He asked the MoS for permission to approach other firms, and the MoS replied on 7 March to say that they had no objections provided he 'apprises them [the firms] of the security aspect'. On 13 March however, the MoS wrote again to Cockerell to tell him that they had been wrong, and he was, in fact, not free to talk about his ideas to anyone. Only the comptroller of patents could give permission, and Cockerell must make a direct application for this (PRO: AVIA65/1804).

Both the MoS and the Admiralty were, in fact, trying their best to get all the secrecy surrounding the hovercraft patents removed. The hold-up was due to the fact that all three patent applications had now been filed in the USA, Canada, and Australia, and requests for secrecy had been made in all cases. This was possible in these three countries only because the wartime arrangements (see Section 8.7) had now been made permanent. As Lord Lucas had said, the 1949 Act made 'permanent the war-time procedure'. This philosophy had been applied widely.

The problem now, as a minute dated 11 March 1958 by the head of patents at the Admiralty explained, was to get mutual agreement from all four patent offices (UK, USA, Canada, and Australia) to remove the prohibition orders (PRO: AVIA65/1804). The inventor would then be free to talk about his work, in confidence, to potential backers, and he would also be free to make patent applications world-wide. By April 1958, things had moved far enough for Cockerell to make a presentation of his work, and the results of the Saunders Roe development work, to the board of the National Research and Development Corporation (NRDC).

The NRDC had been set up, under the first Labour government, by the Development of Inventions Act 1948 (11 & 12 Geo. VI, c. 60). It had the power to borrow capital and invest it in potentially valuable inventions, patenting these world-wide. The income from royalties on these patents then went to the NRDC until all its expenses were recovered. After that, the inventor would receive an agreed share. A number of good ideas, often originating in the universities, were supported by the NRDC in this way.

Cockerell made a good impression on the NRDC board, and they granted £1,000 at once to cover the costs of patent applications abroad. They also promised to consider further support, provided Saunders Roe produced a full report on the development work that had been done so far. This was all done, and the

NRDC took over support for hovercraft development work at Saunders Roe in August 1958 (PRO: AVIA65/1517). The rest of the story is well known. The prototype passenger-carrying hovercraft, SRN1, was designed and built from scratch in only eight months, to be launched in May 1959, and made its first crossing of the English Channel in July (Hogg (1970), 30–6).

10

The Last Secret Patent

10.1   Closed until 2007

The public records that give details of inventions belonging to the 1960s are just beginning to be opened at the time of writing. The last secret patent could be one that is described in a file that is closed until 1994 (PRO: ADM1/22169). This is already indexed as being about the patents of C. C. Mitchell, an aeronautical engineer who had a number of secret patents concerning the hardware used in the Second World War for catapulting aircraft from ships (PRO: ADM1/13839). An example of his work is described in the specification of BPN 649180, which was applied for on 11 October 1938, but not published until 17 January 1951. Apart from the long delay in publication, this specification is not particularly interesting.

The records show that there have been hundreds of secret patent cases since the first case we found in 1855. For most of these cases no technical detail survives, only a record of some agreement. For example, there is a copy of an agreement between one Isaac Francis Taylor and the Admiralty, dated 5 November 1915, according to which Taylor was to produce a full description of his invention, which was 'portable and, in any weather, destroys aircraft of any type which come within a clear range of 25,000 feet' (PRO: TS21/67). Once the Admiralty was satisfied, they were to pay Taylor £500,000, and he undertook to 'obtain and assign to the Government a secret patent for the invention'. The Zeppelin raids on the City of London in September 1915 had caused damage well in excess of £500,000, so Taylor was not setting the stakes too high. Who he was and what hardware he had in mind is not known. It would be possible to cite many such cases from the early nineteenth century up to the present day.

This brings us back to a point that was considered at the end of Chapter 5 and again at the beginning of Chapter 8: the enthusiasm of some men for applying their technical knowledge to war. I make no apology for having frequently referred to an inventor as 'he' in this book. It is, of course, possible to show how women have been able to invent just as well as men (Vare and Ptacek (1988); Moussa (1991)), and in the military field too, but women have not usually been involved in the kind of inventions that were selected by the secret patent filter. On the whole, it has been men who have dominated modern technology in general and military technology in particular (Faulkner and Arnold (1985)).

We have, then, reached the end of the story as far as secret patent cases are concerned. The records of cases more recent that the hovercraft (see Chapter 9) are still closed and are, perhaps, best left secret anyway. There is one recent event, however, that is of interest in the history of secret patents: the passage of the 1977 Patents Act through Parliament. The files containing the confidential papers about the 1977 bill are closed until 2007. For this reason it is easier to look at the final Act first, and then examine what Parliament was up to when the bill was under consideration.

10.2   The Patents Act of 1977

The reforms that the new Patents Act brought in had been proposed by the Banks Committee, which was appointed to examine the patent system and patent law, and had worked from 1967 until 1970. Its report (BPP 1970–1 (4407), xliii. 1) begins with a very valuable review of patent history, a discussion on the value of patents, and an outline of international agreements. The main body of the report is concerned with procedure and law. A short White Paper, *Patent Law Reform*, was printed a few years later to summarize the proposals for change (BPP 1974–5 (6000), xxx. 113).

The new Patents Act 1977 (25 & 26 Eliz. II, c. 37) brought the patent law of the United Kingdom more into line with the Strasbourg Convention and marked a first step towards the international patents of the future. It introduced important reforms concerning employee's patents, putting the employee in a more favourable position with respect to the employer in cases where the employee had made an invention that would not be expected in the normal course of work.

The 'inventive step' was introduced, by the Patents Act of 1977, as an additional requirement for patentability (Beier (1986)). There was also a major change in the way patent applications were dealt with at the Patent Office. The new procedure meant that the applicant's provisional specification was published eighteen months after it was first filed, and the Patent Office examiners added to the title-page of this publication a comprehensive list of all the previous patents, and even previous applications, that had been found to interfere with it. No formal examination of allowability was implied by this: the applicant was simply put into the position of having to decide what changes should be made in the initial application to improve its chances. In many cases the decision was made to abandon the idea of a patent altogether, and this was a far more economical procedure than the old one. Otherwise, the applicant would make amendments and request a formal examination of the amended specification.

This change in procedure brought about a new system of numbering for British patents (*OJ(P)* 4673 at 2941–2) which began on 1 January 1979. Applications made under the new Act began to be published in 1979, and the first one was given the number 2000001A. If the application went ahead and a patent was issued, this would be published using the same number followed by a 'B'. Patents that had been applied for under the old Act of 1949 were still appearing, of course, and these continued to use the old system of numbering that had started in 1916. Very few of these were left by the 1990s: the last old law patent published in 1991 was BPN 1605338.

What did the new Patents Act of 1977 have to say about secrecy? Section 22 of the Act repeated the old procedure, laid down by section 18 of the previous Act of 1949, empowering the comptroller to prohibit publication of information 'predjudicial to the defence of the realm', to which the new Act *added* information 'predjudicial to the safety of the public'. Section 23 of the new Act repeated the restrictions concerning patent applications abroad that had been included in section 18 of the 1949 Act. There was, then, the same, perhaps a little more, secrecy surrounding British patent law after the 1977 Act as there had been before. It may be thought that this happened with the same silent assent of Parliament as had happened in 1859, 1907, and 1949, but that was not the case.

10.3   The 1977 Bill in Parliament

The Patents Bill of 1977 'achieved the doubtful distinction of having had the highest number of amendments tabled against any Act in modern times; over 700 in the House of Lords and over 250 in the House of Commons' (Vitoria (1978), 3). The reason for this may have had more to do with the perilous situation of the Labour government in early 1977 than with the bill itself. The previous year, 1976, had seen spectacular spending cuts by the government, a sterling crisis, and, finally, an appeal to the IMF for a loan, with all the further restrictions that it implied. The Labour government was having a terrible time, and where the opposition could make it even more uncomfortable they naturally did so.

The new Patents Bill was introduced in the House of Lords and had its second reading late in January 1977. The Lords spent many days at work on the bill in committee and were still at it at the end of April. It was then that a contradiction, one that has been lurking in the background throughout this book, emerged and resulted, on 28 April, in two government defeats in the Lords in the space of a few minutes.

The contradiction concerns the case of an inventor who chooses *not* to become involved with the patent system. Such an attitude is understandable in circumstances where the inventor's livelihood does not depend upon patent royalties. The inventor of the late twentieth century will normally be an employee, not a freelance like John Macintosh or William Armstrong in the mid-nineteenth century. New and useful ideas can always find a publisher, and the author will receive acknowledgement and some extra income. To make a patent, on the other hand, is expensive, and there is always the chance that nothing but trouble will come of it. This applies to an invention an employer has no claim on. In the United Kingdom the state has no control at all over publications of this technical kind. If Leo Szilard had known how to make an atomic bomb, and had written a short article for, let us say, *Practical Mechanics*, showing two cylindrical pieces of U^{235} being blown into contact with one another at the centre of a long gun-barrel, closed at both ends, it is very likely that it would have been published. There was, and is, no mechanism of censorship on such publications, except the editor's feelings of good taste and common sense.

This contradiction was aired in the House of Lords on 28 April 1977, when their lordships arrived at clause 20 of the first draft of the new Patents Bill. This clause covered 'Information prejudicial to defence of realm or safety of public' (*PDL* 382 at 708). The Earl of Halsbury questioned the good sense of the secrecy provisions and also wondered about their origin, believing that this must be in the Patents Act of 1907. He had made enquiries, he told their lordships, and had consulted references, and concluded that the secrecy provisions were 'unused, so far as I can determine' until 'the arms race leading up to World War II' (*PDL* 382 at 709). He went on to say: 'We live in a world of uncensored free publication. . . . why do we want to make a quite exceptional type of treatment for publication in the form of a patent?'

Lord Oram, the government whip, replied to the Earl of Halsbury's questions and made it clear that he had no idea why the secrecy clause was in the bill, or where it had come from. Despite this, he said there was 'no question' of changing it in any way (*PDL* 382 at 712–14). Their lordships went on to look at clause 21, which dealt with the prohibition on patent applications abroad, and the same kind of unsatisfactory replies came from the government whip when questions were asked about the reasons for this clause. The Earl of Halsbury, very reasonably, proposed that both clauses 20 and 21 be removed from the bill. If nobody could tell their lordships why the clauses were there, or where they had come from, the clauses had no business to be in the bill. Their lordships agreed. Clause 20 was voted out by 98 to 44 and clause 21 by 92 to 35.

It should be noted that the Earl of Halsbury was in a good position to advise their lordships on this issue. As an independent member, he had no reason to embarrass the government unduly, and he knew about patents from practical experience. He had been managing director of NRDC from its creation, in 1949, until 1959.

The result of all this was that the bill arrived in the House of Commons with no secrecy clauses whatsoever (BPP 1976–7 (122), iii. 451). During the second reading the Under-secretary of State for Trade remarked that 'the Government are concerned about the removal, on the insistance of noble Lords in Opposition, of the secrecy Clauses in the original draft of the Bill. . . . we propose at a later stage to re-instate that provision in the Bill' (*PDC* 932 at 1444).

Reinstatement duly took place when the bill was with Standing Committee D of the House of Commons between 28 June and 5 July 1977. The final form of the bill was printed (BPP 1976–7 (478), iii. 583) with the two clauses, now 22 and 23, back in place.

When the bill went back to the Lords, only twenty-four hours were left before Parliament would be prorogued on 28 July. The Earl of Halsbury remarked upon the reinstatement of the secrecy clauses in the bill. 'We can go on living with it for the time being' (*PDL* 386 at 1057), he observed. The bill received royal assent the next day.

10.4   A Secret Obsession

Why has secrecy been a feature of the British patent system for so long? It is just possible to believe C. M. Clode's fears, in 1864, of giving away secrets to 'foreign powers' (Chapter 3), and we may sympathize with Colonel Clark's attempts, in 1921, to justify his duties 'by the paramount necessity of safeguarding the safety of the Realm' (Chapter 7). In the 1990s, however, it seems sensible to look for a deeper explanation.

When secrecy, in the form of a government prohibition on publication, first appeared in this story, it concerned John Macintosh and his plans to win the war in the Crimea. This exercise resulted in a £1,000 grant to the inventor. In the next case, considered in Chapter 3, William Armstrong's encounter with the British government's obsession with secrecy resulted in a salary of £2,000 per annum for him, backdated for three years. In both cases the inventors were in receipt of considerable rewards. One gave nothing in return, and the other very little: Armstrong resigned his appointment in 1863 when his gun design had to be abandoned and replaced with the earlier muzzle-loading, unrifled, design due to operational difficulties in the field (*EB*11, 2 at 592).

It is possible to get a feel for the value of the rewards that Macintosh and Armstrong received by bearing in mind that £100 per annum was more than enough to support an urban working-class family in the 1850s (*EB*11, 7 at 290). Later in the nineteenth century the tables seem to have been turned, and the government was using secrecy to get the better of inventors, who, by 1869, were 'swarming like hornets about their ears' (Chapter 3). The first Official Secrets Act was passed at a time when an MP could suggest, in the House of Commons, that the Post Office could use the new Act to cover up the fact that it 'pirated' inventions, and, at the same time, the Attorney-General was quite open about secrecy being used to economize at the War Office (Chapter 4).

In Chapter 5 the cases of Marconi and the Wright brothers were considered. These inventors offered secrets to the British government that, we now recognize with hindsight, were the beginnings of two entirely new industries. The offers were not taken up. The case of Marconi is particularly complex, for we have the evidence in his first letter to the War Office that suggests he may have hoped to be taken on, like Louis Brennan had been, 'permanently for the service of the Queen'. The government, however, can be advised on 'secret' technical problems only by its own officials, who have their own careers to consider. In the case of Marconi, Captain Jackson recognized him as a key figure for the future development of radio for the Royal Navy, but he would have wanted Marconi outside the service, in private industry where there was an atmosphere of a free exchange of ideas. No secrets were needed when people had to learn a new craft as difficult as radio in the 1900s. Flight, in the 1920s, was in the same situation.

Moving further into the twentieth century with the later chapters we noted, at the beginning of Chapter 6, that the Secretary of State gave no sensible explanation for the secrecy that was imposed upon the two patents from Lord Rayleigh's Explosives Committee. His explanation, in the House of Commons, was why the patents had been taken out. This made sense, but why were they secret patents? If the patents concerned were any good, the government could have claimed royalties from all kinds of manufacturers, but such a claim is of no value with a patent that can be used only with a government contract. The case is difficult to understand. A royalty claim of a fraction of 1 per cent can earn a formidable income from an industry that makes goods of such a consumable nature as fireworks or ammunition for sporting-guns.

The contradictions continue as we consider the secret patents from between the two world wars. The autopilot secrets had to be opened with haste, the Boulton Paul secrets were only two-thirds closed, and Leo Szilard had no secret, although he used it to good effect. In the Second World War we are back on more familiar ground. Secrecy is the norm in times of war. The interest then is in the people involved, the inventions, and the procedures used. And then, when the war ended, there was the opening of the Great Secret: the atomic bomb. This seemed to cause a reaction in the framing of new patent law, taking it back to an even more secret form than it had a century before. As we saw, at the end of Chapter 7, a far more mature attitude to secrecy had been developing in the fighting departments just before the Second World War. There was every reason to expect the secrecy clauses to disappear from the next patents bill but, instead, secrecy was strengthened in 1949 and again in 1977.

There has been one more opportunity since 1977 to get rid of the secrecy attached to British patent law. This was when the Copyright, Designs and Patents Act of 1988 was going through Parliament. No changes were made. Sections 22 and 23 of the Patents Act 1977 remain statutes in force. Every issue of the Patent Office *Journal* carries the 'Notice to Inventors' first introduced in 1922 (Chapter 6), now calling their attention to section 23, which prohibits UK residents applying for patents abroad before applying at home.

In modern times, when patents are international and are the affairs of multinational enterprises, why does this potential for secrecy remain? The modern patent system is only one sector of the industrial and intellectual property market that employs thousands of people world-wide. It has grown to be this size over the past 150 years, and during that time the importance and meaning of patents has changed in very complicated ways. Today patents mean different things to different industries. The pharmaceutical industry attaches great importance to its patents; aerospace finds patents relatively unimportant; and the electronics industry lies somewhere in between the two extremes (von Hippel (1988), 53; Kingston (1984), 79–92). But it is generally agreed that patents are not useful for excluding imitators or for capturing royalty income (von Hippel (1988), 47). Trade marks, on the other hand, are vital in this respect (Kingston (1984), 92–5) and so are trade secrets, for which there is 'a well-developed law . . . unequivocally on the side of the secret owner' (ibid. 86). This last point is important because it brings out a contradiction between the patent law and the laws that govern commercial secrecy. As David Vaver has pointed out:

patents and copyrights are supposed to encourage work to be disclosed to the public and thus to increase society's pool of ideas and knowledge. Yet many inventions are kept secret and the law rigorously protects that decision, whether or not disclosure would be more socially useful than secrecy (Vaver (1991), 127).

What, then, is the function of the patent system today? The 'incentive to invent' argument, which we saw Sir William Armstrong casting doubts upon in 1864 (Section 3.3), is almost taken for granted by modern economists of the neoclassical or marginalist schools. Wyatt, for example, in his *Economics of Invention*, assumes that what he terms 'endogenous invention', that is inventive activity strongly influenced by economic forces, is the accepted model for understanding such social behaviour (Wyatt (1986), 147–8). Posner, in his *Economic Analysis of Law*, is definitive on the incentive question: 'the law could decide not to recognize property rights in ideas, but then too few ideas would be discovered' (Posner (1986), 36–7).

Some authors have tried to get some real facts on the question of patents acting as incentives to invent. A very interesting example is the work of Schiff (1971) who looked at the records for the Netherlands, over the period 1869–1912, and Switzerland, from 1850 to 1907. These were the periods during which both countries had no patent system at all. Schiff's conclusions are that the Netherlands and Switzerland stood up well in comparison with other countries when it came to speed of industrialization and attracting foreign investment. As far as inventive activity was concerned, the Netherlands seems to have been somewhat behind, but Switzerland was very much in the forefront. Both countries came back into the international patent community because they felt left out of things, and there was a possibility of sanctions from the International Union for the Protection of Industrial Property (IUPIP). After all, the citizens of both countries were making good use of other countries' patent systems.

For the twentieth century, Jewkes, Sawers, and Stillerman (1969) have looked at a large number of case histories in all fields of invention. They conclude that the whole question of what may or may not foster invention and innovation is still open, and that the problem is 'much more complicated than was ever imagined by those who have dominated opinion and influenced public policy upon these matters in recent years' (p. 226). Work in this area is, of course, extremely difficult: there is no point in asking the inventors for their opinion. The whole concept of induced invention has also been questioned by Nordhaus (1973) on theoretical grounds.

For the economic influence of the patent system, empirical research is far easier. Is there any financial gain for a large corporation in taking out patents? All large firms are able to show not only considerable income from their patents, but also a large expenditure on patent litigation, patent agents, and, more than anything, payments for the patent rights of other very large firms. The facts about this have been collected by von Hippel (1988, pp. 47–53) who shows that industry in the United Kingdom during 1968 earned only a few per cent of its total research and development costs from patent royalties. Von Hippel tabulates research and development costs, royalty income, patent costs, and total sales for a whole range of industries. In 1968 the growth of the multinational company was only just beginning. A similar study today might show an even better balance between patent income and patent costs, because manufacturing in the less developed countries is more under the control of very large multinational concerns. These could well be transferring money from the periphery to the centre under the heading of 'royalty payments', but it may be difficult to discover what such transfers mean.

Patent agreements and cross-licensing agreements provide a system of control and information flow across industry that is vital to its operation (von Hippel (1988), 51; Kingston (1984), 90–1). This system could have been set up by the big firms with simple agreements under the law of contract, but it has developed through using the patent law and the services of all the patent courts and patent agents already involved. This means that the system is open to others: to individuals, small firms, and governments.

It is possible that the UK secret patent system started with the hope that the government, which in the nineteenth century owned some major manufacturing plant in the form of ordnance factories, would get a better deal in some way. Today, it continues in the hope that the government may get an entrée to the international system of control and information, set up by the patent system, on better terms than other users. If these were the hopes of the government, all the evidence suggests that the secret patent system has been as unhelpful in the twentieth century as it was in the nineteenth.

Following the secret patent thread through the history of patents may have been of some help in showing us how we have arrived at the very complex patent system we have today. Perhaps it has also been helpful in bringing the question of intellectual property to the forefront. The concept of saleable property in ideas is surely dubious when the idea is held as a 'secret' by one person, and then found to be common knowledge. It is similarly highlighted as invalid when the 'secret' is found to be misunderstood by the person who claims the property rights.

So often questioned in the nineteenth century, the idea of intellectual property is now, at the end of the twentieth century, firmly established. We have at last arrived at the time the young Karl Marx foresaw:

> when the very things which till then had been communicated, but never exchanged; given, but never sold; acquired, but never bought—virtue, love, conviction, knowledge, conscience, etc.—when everything finally passed into commerce. . . . the time when everything, moral or physical, having become a marketable value, is brought to the market to be assessed at its truest value (MECW (1976), 113).

List of References

Aitken, J. (1971). *Officially Secret*. Weidenfeld & Nicolson, London.

Alekseev, N. F., and Malyarov, D. E. (1940). 'Poluchenie moshchnykh kolebanii magnetronom v santimetrovom diapazone voln'. *Journal of Technical Physics*, 10, 1297–300.

Amyot, J. R. (1989). *Hovercraft Technology, Economics and Applications*. Elsevier, Amsterdam.

Andrew, C. (1985). *Secret Service: The Making of the British Intelligence Community*. Heinemann, London.

Baker, W. J. (1970). *A History of the Marconi Company*. Methuen, London.

Barrett-Lennard, T. (1908). *An Account of the Families of Lennard and Barrett*. Privately printed.

Beier, F.-K. (1986). 'The Inventive Step in its Historical Development'. *IIC (International Review of Industrial Property and Copyright Law)*, 17, 301–23.

Blanco-White, T. A., and Jacob, R. (1986). *Patents, Trade Marks, Copyright and Industrial Designs*. Sweet & Maxwell, London.

Boot, H. A. H., and Randall, J. T. (1976). 'Historical Note on the Cavity Magnetron'. *Institute of Electrical and Electronics Engineers. Transactions on Electronic Devices*, ED-23, 724–9.

Bowen, E. G. (1987). *Radar Days*. Adam Hilger, Bristol.

Burns, R. W. (1988). *Radar Developments to 1945*. Peter Peregrinus, London.

Cantrell, J. A. (1984). *James Nasmyth and the Bridgewater Foundry*. Manchester Univ. Press, Manchester.

Clunn, H. P. (1932). *The Face of London*. Simpkin Marshall, London.

Collins, G. B. (1948). *Microwave Magnetrons*. McGraw-Hill, New York.

Constant, E. W. (1980). *The Origins of the Turbo-jet Revolution*. Johns Hopkins Univ. Press, Baltimore.

Cooper, A. W. (1982). *The Men who Breached the Dams*. William Kimber, London.

Cornish, W. R. (1989). *Intellectual Property*. Second edn. Sweet & Maxwell, London.

Crouch, T. (1989). *The Bishop's Boys*. W. W. Norton, New York.

Davis, N. P. (1969). *Lawrence and Oppenheimer*. Jonathan Cape, London.

Dickens, C. (1986). *The Pickwick Papers*. Penguin, London.

Disraeli, B. (1989). *Coningsby*. Penguin, London.

Dougan, D. (1970). *The Great Gun-maker*. Frank Graham, Newcastle upon Tyne.

Dutton, H. I. (1984). *The Patent System and Inventive Activity during the Industrial Revolution 1750–1852*. Manchester Univ. Press, Manchester.

Easlea, B. (1980). *Witch-hunting, Magic and the New Philosophy*. Harvester, Brighton.

—— (1981). *Science and Sexual Oppression*. Weidenfeld & Nicolson, London.

—— (1983). *Fathering the Unthinkable*. Pluto, London.

Faulkner, W., and Arnold, E. (eds.) (1985). *Smothered by Invention: Technology in Women's Lives*. Pluto, London.

Feld, B. T., and Szilard, G. W. (1972) (eds.). *The Collected Works of Leo Szilard*. MIT Press, Cambridge, Mass.

Gomme, A. A. (1946). *Patents of Inventions*. Longman, London.

Gowing, M. (1974). *Independence and Deterrence*. 2 vols. Macmillan, London.

Gray, E. (1975). *The Devil's Device*. Seely, Service, London.

Harding, H. (1953). *Patent Office Centenary*. HMSO, London.

Heims, S. J. (1980). *John von Neumann and Norbert Wiener*. MIT Press, Cambridge, Mass.

Hinsley, F. H. (1979). *British Intelligence in the Second World War*, vol. i. HMSO, London.

—— and Stripp, A. (eds.) (1993). *Codebreakers: The Inside Story of Bletchley Park*. Oxford University Press, Oxford.

von Hippel, E. (1988). *The Sources of Invention*. Oxford University Press, Oxford.

Hodges, A. (1983). *Alan Turing: The Enigma*. Hutchinson, London.

Hogg, G. (1970). *The Hovercraft Story*. Abelard-Schuman, London.

Hooper, D. (1987). *Official Secrets: The Use and Abuse of the Act*. Secker & Warburg, London.

Howard, F. (1988). *Wilbur and Orville*. Robert Hale, London.

Jewkes, J., Sawers, D., and Stillerman, R. (1969). *The Sources of Invention*. Macmillan, London.

Jolly, W. P. (1972). *Marconi*. Constable, London.

Jungk, R. (1958). *Brighter than a Thousand Suns*. Gollancz, London.

Kelly, F. C. (1943). *The Wright Brothers*. Harcourt, New York.

Kingston, W. (1984). *The Political Economy of Innovation*. Martinus Nijhoff, The Hague.

Lee, S. (ed.) (1896). *Dictionary of National Biography*. Smith, Elder, London.

Macfie, R. A. (1883). *Copyright and Patents for Inventions*, vol. ii. Clark, Edinburgh.

References

Machlup, F., and Penrose, E. (1950). 'The Patent Controversy in the Nineteenth Century'. *Journal of Economic Hist.*, 10/1, 1–29.

Mackenzie, K. (1968). *The English Parliament*. Penguin, London.

McKenzie, P. (1983). *W. G. Armstrong*. Longhirst, Newcastle upon Tyne.

MacLeod, C. (1988). *Inventing the Industrial Revolution: The English Patent System 1660–1800*. Cambridge Univ. Press, Cambridge.

Marconi, D. (1962). *My Father Marconi*. Frederick Muller, London.

MECW (1976). *Karl Marx and Frederick Engels. The Collected Works*. Vol. vi: *Marx and Engels: 1845–1848*. Lawrence & Wishart, London.

Megaw, E. C. S. (1946). 'The High Power Pulsed Magnetron: A Review of Early Developments'. *Journal of the Institution of Electrical Engineers*, 93, 3A/5, 977–84.

Merton, R. K. (1973). *The Sociology of Science*. Univ. of Chicago Press, Chicago.

Mill, J. S. (1926). *Principles of Political Economy*. Longmans, Green, London.

Moussa, F. (1991). *Women Inventors*. Moussa, Geneva.

Nordhaus, W. D. (1973). 'Some Skeptical Thoughts on the Theory of Induced Invention'. *Quarterly Journal of Economics*, 87/2, 208–19.

Ogburn, W. F., and Thomas, D. (1922). 'Are Inventions Inevitable?'. *Political Science Quarterly*, 37/1, 83–98.

Okabe, K. (1930). 'Amplification and Detection of Ultra-short Waves'. *Proceedings of the Institute of Radio Engineers*, 18, 1028–37.

Parsons, R. H. (1939). *The Early Days of the Power Station Industry*. Cambridge Univ. Press, Cambridge.

Phillips, J. (1984). *Charles Dickens and the Poor Man's Tale of a Patent*. ESC Publications, Oxford.

Posner, R. (1986). *Economic Analysis of Law*. Third edn. Little Brown, Boston.

Pringle, P., and Spigelman, J. (1982). *The Nuclear Barons*. Michael Joseph, London.

Resek, C. (ed.) (1964). *War and the Intellectuals: Essays by Randolph S. Bourne*. Harper & Row, New York.

Rolph, P. M. (1991). *Fifty Years of the Cavity Magnetron*. Univ. of Birmingham, Birmingham.

Samuel, A. L. (1936). *Electron Discharge Device*. US Patent No. 2063342.

Schiff, E. (1971). *Industrialization without National Patents*. Princeton Univ. Press, Princeton, NJ.

Siemens, W. (1966). *Inventor and Entrepreneur*. Lund Humphries, London.

Thomas, R. M. (1991). *Espionage and Secrecy: The Official Secrets Acts 1911–1989*. Routledge, London.

Trillo, R. L. (1992–3). *Jane's High-Speed Marine Craft*. Twenty-fifth edn. Jane's Information Group, Coulsdon.

Van Zyl Smit, D. (1985). 'Professional Patent Agents and the Development of the English Patent System'. *International Journal of Sociology and Law*, 13, 79–105.

Vare, E. A., and Ptacek, G. (1988). *Mothers of Invention*. Morrow, New York.

Vaver, D. (1991). 'Some Agnostic Observations on Intellectual Property'. *Intellectual Property Journal*, 6/2, 125–53.

Vitoria, M. (ed.) (1978). *The Patents Act 1977*. Sweet & Maxwell, London.

Walford, E. (1987). *Old London: Strand to Soho*. Alderman, London.

Watt, R. A. W. (1957). *Three Steps to Victory*. Odhams, London.

Weart, S. R., and Szilard, G. W. (1978). *Leo Szilard: His Version of the Facts*. MIT Press, Cambridge, Mass.

Webster, C., and Frankland, N. (1961). *The Strategic Air Offensive against Germany 1939–45*, vol. iii. HMSO, London.

Williams, D. (1965). *Not in the Public Interest*. Hutchinson, London.

Wyatt, G. (1986). *The Economics of Invention*. Harvester, Brighton.

Index

Abel, F. 38, 44
Aberdeen 72
abolitionists 25, 32, 34
abridgements 65, 66
Admiralty 27, 35, 44, 69, 75, 100,
  120
  contracts 104
  DRPP 124
  DSR 95, 104
  and inventions 26, 30, 71, 80, 95,
    129
  patents 23, 47, 91, 97, 127
  Stop List 125
Air Inventions Committee 72
Air Ministry 68, 72, 75, 85, 91, 117
  DSR 98
  and inventions 72, 80
  patents 91, 97
  secrets 76, 114
Aitken, J. 44
Aldershot 84
Aldershot 76
Alderson, H. J. 46
Alekseev, N. F. 101, 107
Alverstone, Lord 63
Amyot, J. R. 123
Andrew, C. 45, 59
Appleton, E. 97
Armstrong, W. 20–4, 36, 132, 134,
  137
Arnold, E. 130
Ashley, P. 81
Aston, F. W. 113
atomic bomb 90, 111, 117, 132, 135
atomic energy 113, 115
Atomic Energy Act (1946) 115–120
Attle, C. 116
Attorney-General 5, 12, 18, 26, 45
Australia 104, 127
autopilot 84

Babbage, C. 31
Bacon, F. 112
Baker, W. J. 49, 50, 51, 52, 53
Baldwin, S. 94

Balfour, G. 66
Banks Committee 130
Bannister, C. G. 8
Barrett-Lennard, T. 11
Beier, F.-K. 130
Belgium 25
Bessemer, H. 32–3
Bikini Atoll 114
Birkbeck, G. 10
Birmingham 17, 100, 105–6
von Bismarck, O. 25
Blanco-White, T. A. 32
Bletchley 111–12
Board of Trade 68, 80, 119
  1900 Committee 63, 65, 66
  President of 14, 40, 69, 98, 121
boffins 95
Boot, H. A. H. 100, 102, 105–7
Boulton Paul Co. 86, 135
Bourne, R. S. 95
Bowen, E. G. 99
breech loading 24
Brennan, L. 52–3, 135
Bridgewater 33
Bright, J. 16
British Airways 85
Brougham, Lord 13, 14, 16
Brunel, I. K. & M. I. 12, 15
Burns, R. W. 99, 101
Bulter, R. A. 97

Campbell, F. A. 36
Cameron, C. 45
Canada 104, 127
Cantrell, J. A. 33
Carson, E. 63
catapulting aircraft 129
Cavendish Laboratory 104
Chalmers, T. A. 89
Chamberlain, J. 40–1
Chancery Lane 10, 18
Chapman, H. M. 46
Churchill, W. 117
Clarendon Laboratory 89
Clark, W. H. D. 81–4, 134

Clode, C. M. 20, 24, 36–8, 40, 43, 134
Clunn, H. P. 49
Cobden, R. 16
Cockburn, A. 27
Cockerell, C. S. 123–7
coherer 53–7
Collins, G. B. 108
commercial secrets 34, 136
common law 19
computing gunsight 87
conscientious objectors 35
Conservative Party 20
Constant, E. W. 48
Cooke, P. A. 84, 86
Cooper, A. W. 108
copyright 30–2
Cornish, W. R. 31
Creuzot-Loire 33
Crimean War 8, 36
Cripps, S. 98–9
Crookes, W. 62
Crouch, T. 59
cryptography 111

Dale, H. 97
Dalton, C. N. 64–5, 67–8, 70, 122
dambusters 108–11
Davis, N. P. 100, 114
defence regulations 71, 72, 96, 97,
    105, 115, 120
Derby, Earl 16, 18, 22
Development of Inventions Act
    (1948) 127
Dewar, J. 38, 44
Dickens, C. 10, 13
Director of Public Prosecutions 74
Disraeli, B. 20, 40
DORA 71, 96
Dougan, D. 23
Douglas, H. 23–4
DSIR 79–81
Dutton, H. I. 2, 10, 11, 12

Easlea, B. 60
Edinburgh 25
Egypt 124
Einstein, A. 61, 90
electoral laws 13
Engels, F. 39
English Electric Co. 124
Enterprise 27
examiners 2, 17, 40–1, 57–8, 63–7
Explosives Committee 62, 135

Farey, J. 11–12
Farnborough 84
Faulkner, W. 130
Feather, R. B. 26–30, 38, 43, 47, 56
Feld, B. T. 89, 90
France 11, 33, 38, 124
Frankland, N. 108, 111
Franks, W. T. 71–3, 81, 105
free trader 15, 19, 32
Fry, E. 63–4
Fuchs, K. 36
fuse 22

GEC 102–3
German chemical industry 69
Germany 33, 38, 90, 108, 111, 125
Gladstone, W. E. 32, 40
Gleichen, E. 59
Godley, Mr. 36–7
Gomme, A. A. 15, 25
Gowing, M. 117
Granville, Lord 14–17
Graphic 85
Gray, E. 52
Great Exhibition 13
Grey, Earl 13
Griffiths, R. 23
gun turrets 91
gyromagnetic frequency 101

Hahn, O. 113
Halifax, Lord 104
Halsbury, Earl 123, 132–4
Harding, H. 65
Hardy, T. 49
Hazelton, G. 82
Heims, S. J. 60
Hinsley, F. H. 112
von Hippel, E. 136, 138
Hiroshima 113, 116
Hodges, A. 112
Hodgskin, T. 10
Hogg, G. 123, 128
Holywell Street 64
Hooper, D. 44
Hoover Constellation 126
Houldsworth, W. 66
hovercraft 123–8
Howard, F. 59, 60

Illustrated London News 85
IMF 132
Imperial Airways 85

Imrie, N. D. 125
incentive to invent 15, 23, 137
intellectual property 5, 15, 24, 30, 136, 138
  rights 24, 31, 37–8, 76, 99
interdepartmental committee (1906) 67
  (1920) 80–4
interdepartmental conference (1921) 74
interference 67
inventive step 22, 26, 31, 53, 55, 56, 130
Ireland 18, 94
isotopes 72, 113
Israel 124
Italy 94, 125
IUPIP 137

Jackson, H. 57, 135
Jacob, R. 32
Japan 101, 113
Jewkes, J. 137
Jolly, W. P. 49, 50, 53, 57, 58, 61
Jungk, R. 88, 113

Kelly, F. 19
Kelly, F. C. 59
Kingston, W. 23, 136, 138
klystron 100
Kronstadt 8

Labour Party 94, 116, 132
Lambrich, R. 109
Lansdowne, Marquess 51
Lee, S. 15
Lefroy, J. H. 24
Lennard, T. B. 11
Liberal Party 32, 40
Lindemann, F. A. 89
Lloyd-George, D. 69
Lloyd, J. H. 15
Lodge, O. 57
London Mechanics' Institute 10
Lord Chancellor 5–9, 17, 36, 40, 57
Lucas, Lord 121

Macfie, R. A. 25–7, 30, 32, 33
Maclup, F. 25, 34
Macintosh, J. 4–9, 18, 56, 132, 134
Mackenzie, K. 70
McKenzie, P. 23
MacLeod, C. 2

McMahon Act 114
magnetron 100–8
Malyarov, D. E. 101, 107
Manhattan Project 106, 114
man-trap 64
Marconi Company 50, 58, 97, 124
Marconi, D. 49, 50
Marconi, G. 49–58, 135
market 15, 139
Marmonier Fils 84
Martin, A. J. 68, 75
Marx, K. 139
May, C. 15
Mechanics' Magazine 8, 10, 11, 19
Megaw, E. C. S. 102, 105
Medical Research Council 80
Meredith, F. W. 84, 86
Merton, R. K. 22
MI6 59
Mill, J. S. 30, 31, 32
Million Fund 79–80
Ministry of Supply 117, 120, 122, 125–7
Mitchell, C. C. 129
Moulton, J. F. 62, 72
Mountbatten, Lord 124
Moussa, F. 130
Muntz, G. F. 17

Nagasaki 113
Napoleon, L. 16
Nasmyth, J. 33
Nature 80
Netherlands 25, 137
von Neumann, J. 60
Nicholson, W. F. 76
Noddack, I. 113
Nordhaus, W. D. 137
Notice to Inventors 75, 136
NRDC 98, 126–8, 133

Official Secrets Act (1889) 35, 44, 47, 68, 134
  (1911) 44, 68
  (1920) 44, 68, 74
  (1939) 44
  (1989) 44
Ogburn, W. F. 22
Okabe, K. 100
Oliphant, M. L. E. 100
Oppenheimer, R. 114
Oram, Lord 133
ordinance factories 39, 42, 138

Paddington 49
Palmer, R. 16, 17, 26, 27, 29, 41
Palmer, W. 98
Parsons, C. A. 80
Parsons, R. H. 50
patent
  agents 11, 12, 19, 34, 56, 104, 124, 138
  history 2
  law 15, 17, 22, 30, 40
  litigation 138
  numbers 82, 131
Patent Office 2, 4, 9, 34, 64, 123
  administrative secrets 25
  building 18, 34, 48
  Comptroller 41, 67, 68, 70–4, 82, 127
  confidentiality 47, 74, 122
  Journal 4, 63, 65, 75, 86, 106, 136
  library 5, 17, 34, 48
  rules 70
Patents Act (1835) 13, 27
  (1852) 4, 9, 17, 27, 33
  (1859) 19, 24, 36, 43, 119
  (1883) 35, 38, 40–4, 64
  (1902) 66
  (1907) 69, 83, 97, 117, 119, 133
  (1949) 109, 121, 125, 127, 131
  (1977) 82, 130–4
  (1988) 136
Peel, R. 11, 32
Penrose, E. 25, 34
Phillips, J. 10
Pickles, E. L. 78, 86
Poole, M. 12
Posner, R. 137
Post Office 44, 50, 80, 98
Preece, W. 50, 53
Pringle, P. 114, 117
Privy Council 79
Prussia 25
Ptacek, G. 130
Public Record Office 35, 46, 67, 129
Pye, D. F. 98

Queen Anne's Gate 126
de Quincey, T. 31

radar 99
RAE 84
Rae, J. 31

Randall, J. T. 100–2, 107
Ranger, J. 118
Rayleigh, Lord 62, 135
real estate 37
Redmond, J. & W. 62
remote control 50, 52
Research Associations 80
Resek, C. 95
Ricardo, D. & J. L. 15, 31
rifled ordinance 20, 24, 40
RNSS 125
Roberts, W. 62
Roe, A. V. 76
Rolph, P. M. 99
Roosevelt, President 90, 104
Royal Commission (1864) 22
  on Awards to Inventors 106
Russel, Lord 13, 16

Sale, M. T. 44
Salisbury, Marquis 62, 66
Samuel, A. L. 101
Saunders, H. 120
Saunders Roe 126–8
Sawers, D. 137
Sayers, J. 100, 105–7
Schiff, E. 137
Scientific Advisory Committee 97
Scotland 18
Secret Patents Committee 70, 91
Select Committee (1829) 11
  (1851) 15
  (1871–2) 32–4, 36
Sevastopol 8
Sheffield 33
Sibthorp, Col. 14
Siemens, K. W. & W. 33
Smith, A. 31
Smith's Instruments Ltd. 86
Soddy, F. 72
Solicitor-General 5, 8, 18, 64
Somerlyton, Lord 124
Somerset, Duke 23
Spencer, Col. 71
Sperry Gyroscope Co. 84
Spigelman, J. 114, 117
Spithead 35
Stalingrad 97
Stanley, Lord 22, 30
Statute of Monopolies 10, 27, 83
steam hammer 33
Stillerman, R. 137
Strassmann, F. 113

Stripp, A. 112
Suez 124
Sverdlov 35
Swann, K. R. 119
Switzerland 25, 137
systems engineer 56, 59
Szilard, G. W. 89, 90
Szilard, L. 3, 88–90, 104, 132, 135

Tallboy 111
Taylor, I. F. 129
Thomas, D. 22
Thomas, R. M. 44, 68
Thompson, S. P. 57
Tirpitz, the 111
torpedo 51, 52
Tory Party 94
trade marks 136
Treasury 98
  Solicitor 68, 120
Trillo, R. L. 123
Truman, President 90, 114
Turing, A. 112

United Kingdom 10, 16–18, 71, 84,
    94, 124
  Atomic Energy Authority 118
United States
  Atomic Energy Commission 114
  Congress 114
  patent law 41

Patent Office 40, 127
  secret patents 104
USSR 101, 107, 108

Van Zyl Smit, D. 11, 12
Vare, E. A. 130
Vaver, D. 136
Vitoria, M. 132

Wallis, B. 108–11
Walford, E. 64
War Office 40, 44, 50, 75, 78
  conference 43, 67
  consultants 62
  and inventions 26, 71, 80
  patents 43, 91
  Solicitor 8, 20, 24, 36, 37
  visitor 52
Washington 104
Watt, R. A. W. 99
Weart, S. R. 89
Webster, C. 108, 111
Westbourne Park 49
Whig Party 11, 19, 27, 32, 94
Wiener, N. 60
Williams, D. 44
Wilson, H. 121
wireless telegraphy 49
Woolwich 39, 84
Wright, C. S. 89, 104, 108, 124
Wright, O. & W. 58–60, 135
Wyatt, G. 137